Daphne Spyropoulos is   , a neuropsychology extern
at Yale Neurology, an advanced practicum student at the
Integrated Brain Health Clinic at Massachusetts General
Hospital/Harvard Medical School, and a Counseling
Psychology PhD candidate at Fordham University in New
York City. She is passionate about the gut-brain axis and the
effects of the gut microbiome on neurodegenerative diseases
and on mood disorders. She has published three fiction books
in Greek.

To Kae

Daphne Spyropoulos

BRAIN'S GOT THE SH*TS AGAIN

Finding Joy and Some Purpose Along The Gut Brain Axis

AUSTIN MACAULEY PUBLISHERS™

LONDON • CAMBRIDGE • NEW YORK • SHARJAH

A CIP catalogue record for this title is available from the British Library.

ISBN 9781398464087 (Paperback)
ISBN 9781398464094 (ePub e-book)

www.austinmacauley.com

First Published 2022
Austin Macauley Publishers Ltd®
1 Canada Square
Canary Wharf
London
E14 5AA

Table of Contents

Chapter 1
Introduction

A few years ago, on a gloomy New York morning, I was sitting in my tiny dorm room on East 35th street, skimming through Ted Talks. Twenty minutes in, a graceful, Finnish doctor appeared on the screen, tall and well-groomed, to explain her fascination with the human anus. She then went on to describe how there is an innate intelligence in our bodies' last bastion, dictating the progression of events in a way that may even be socially acceptable.

To put it in simpler words: your butt knows when you can't go, so it holds tight until it's time.

At least sometimes.

Little did I know at the time, as a Psych PhD student, that the butt-brain, sorry, the gut-brain axis would become my own source of fascination during the next few years. Now, I've always been averse to intense psychoanalytic theories, but when I told one of my professors about my research, they said, "I always knew you had an anal personality!" It was kismet. I am not sure how you got a hold of this book. Perhaps you got it as a birthday gift from your friend who thought the title matched your energy (oops) or your aunt who tried to crack you up after a bad breakup. Glad, you're here and glad, they bought it anyway!

To officially introduce myself, I am Daphne, a Greek-American Psych(o) PhD student living in New York, and I, too, am fascinated by the human anus. Just kidding! Wanted to make a grand entrance. Let's try this again. I am Daphne, a Psych PhD student whose brain had the shits for years and years until a vastly uneventful Euro trip on a winter break, some smokes in Amsterdam, and a bunch of hurting bones.

Yes, joint pain was, in fact, the leeway to the long, slimy, disgusting beauty that is the human gut. Pre-Amsterdam, I had experienced years of intense fatigue that made me cancel most of my social plans (all my friends can attest to that, and they know my car tires couldn't have been that fragile). The chronic fatigue also made me develop compensatory strategies such as mind games and tricks that would convince me to get up and stay up for longer amounts of time.

Two years in the tiredness, my mom took us on a road trip across Spain that helped me realise what I was giving up through surrendering to the exhaustion. Slowly after that, I introduced more travel, internships abroad, and even some fashion modelling into my schedule. I had realised that I would have a tired life, but I was adamant that it would be a full and exciting one. During my Masters' studies, I presented my work at conferences in Mexico City, London, Lisbon, Turkey. I worked at a Psychiatric Hospital in South Africa. I visited Vietnam and Cambodia, all while being a professional clothes' hanger (a hangry one too).

The fatigue was unyielding, and during my first year as a PhD student in New York, I decided to write a 'fiction' book that was actually very autobiographical, about how I was experiencing life and how I thought it was or wasn't affecting my work as a therapist in training. The book was published, I lost some friends and made some new ones, and then I visited my twin brother who was living in Rotterdam.

Tired or not, it is a family rule that when we travel, we walk like savages, and so we did, every day around the Netherlands. A couple of days later, we were on a train to Belgium (got to love Europe!), and I began experiencing intense joint pain across my body. The pain persisted, I flew back to New York, booked an appointment with a rheumatologist at NYU Langone, Covid happened, I flew to Greece and missed the appointment.

A few months after quarantine, when we were allowed to make doctors' appointments, I went to some Greek doctors who eventually diagnosed me with Celiac disease along with a heavy dairy intolerance and a soy throat-closing allergy. "This is silly," I thought, but I decided to give up on my favourite ice cream, chocolate, and snacks that once brightened up my days, just to see if the joint pain would subside.

I promise to anyone who's listening that two days in, my pain had vanished, and so had my fatigue. I AM NOT KIDDING. This was a ten-year companion who had suddenly left the building. Gone. So had my brain-fog. I thought this must have been a coincidence, that the cloud would return the next morning, but it didn't, and it hasn't ever since. Not only that, but my thoughts began being happier, and so did my memories.

As a tired person, my mind would ruminate on negative events, critical comments, and fret about the future. As a celiac, life-averse, tastebuds-doomed person, though, I kept getting these flashbacks of being a happy, young child in our beach house, having enjoyed a good hide-and-seek game with friends, ready to sleep. As I was describing this to my brother, asking him if that's how his own mind worked naturally, he took my face in his palms, starred me in the eye, and said, "What did you take? I won't tell Mom."

I was sure that getting three gut-related diagnoses may not resolve one's physical and mental health problems in a day, as was my case, but I was also curious about what on earth the connection between gut and brain health was, and I knew that it would be my next passion project. As I was describing this to one of my mentors, they warned me that I was wasting my time, but as you may have grasped, I've wasted so much time already, and I am not afraid to do it again.

Before I move on to explain how this book is structured, I must say that I am an avid reader and admirer of Elizabeth Gilbert's stance on creativity. She says that creativity taps you on the shoulder in the form of a "psssst, you", and that ideas float in the universe, asking different people, "Will you be my mother, will you be my father?"

Hell yeah, Liz! When this shitster tapped me on the shoulder, I was ready to dive right in (okay, I hear it now). I spent my summer getting a Nutritional Psychology certification, and then, when it was time to find a clinical placement, I decided to google the most esteemed neuropsychiatric teaching hospital in Greece. The only email address I was able to find was that of the neuropsychology lab director to who I wrote and who invited me in for an interview.

It took me twenty minutes to prep for a job interview that I was greatly unqualified for, and my line of thinking was the following: I only know of neuropsych what we've been taught in school, but if I can find a connection between neurology and the gut-brain axis, then I'm golden. And so I googled 'the enteric nervous system', and my hunch was validated, and I read three academic abstracts, and I marched into that kind man's office, tan and apprehensive, ready to claim my training spot.

The director asked me about my clinical experience and my research interest, and when I mentioned the gut-brain axis and the enteric nervous system, he jumped out of his chair and said, "That is genius! The human body is a tube! All we are is a tube! You're in, we're starting tomorrow." The next morning I began seeing patients with different diagnoses, from Neurosarcoidosis to Multiple Sclerosis, Parkinson's, Alzheimer's, and anything else I could imagine.

A few weeks later, my grandma called and said she had watched a tv interview of a top-rated medical doctor who had been a professor of endocrinology in the States and who ranked as one of the 200 best scientists in the world. He was talking about the effects of sugar on the brain and he mentioned he had a medical practice in Athens. My grandma is a very persistent lady, and she grilled me to email his team and ask to become a part of it. I emailed just to screenshot the message, send it to her and then get back to my peace, but I heard back from them within the week and joined their research endeavours immediately after. We researched osteosarcopenic obesity, how sugar in breast milk could cause myelination in multiple sclerosis patients and other, fascinating topics that I had no idea I would ever get to lay my hands on.

I then joined a memory disorder centre, and I realised soon after that this idea, the gut-brain one, was helping me make it. In the following year, this idea granted me a prestigious fellowship, interviews, and neuropsych externship offers from notable hospitals in New York, including Columbia, Yale, Lenox Hill, Mount Sinai, and Memorial Sloan Kettering. Now let's get back to business, dear reader. If your brain's got the shits again, if you're interested in the effects of the gut on our mental and our neurological health, this book will give you a series of (hopefully) funny stories that will convey to you all I've gathered. It is a sequence of paraboles, true and untrue stories, in an exploration of the gross tube of dreams and faeces that has landed me magical spots of neuropsychological training and a very catchy dinner ice breaker (if you want to call dibs on appetizers that is).

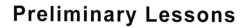

Preliminary Lessons

Chapter 2
The Gut-Brain Axis as a
Vegan's Hellhole

A few years ago, in a systemic therapy class, we were asked to role-play a family. I chose to be the grandmother for which I copy-catted my own, who first went to dental and then to medical school and whose achievements will be shaming the rest of us for years to come. When I mentioned my / my grandmother's qualifications, the professor said, "Where did this grandma come from? Her grandchildren would need to get a PhD in America, and that wouldn't even cut it." To be fair, I am getting my PhD in America, and I do feel like it isn't cutting it.

But when my grandma went to medical school in the 1960s, she wasn't the only woman there. She had a classmate named Voula, whose dad was the village priest in a small Aegean island and who was scandalised when male professors would look at her. Voula was second in her class, right after grams (okay, I'll throw in another Masters in the next few years). She wanted to find a good man – probably a med student – to marry, yet she did not like to date down, and she was the smartest amongst her colleagues.

Voula was adamant about never watering down her wit to be likeable or attractive. She also didn't enjoy being unnoticed. When a gastroenterology professor skipped by her when she was trying to answer how long the human gut is, she stood up. "Excuse me," said the professor, and oh, did she not.

"Excuse you, but I want to give my answer," said Voula, and the professor turned his back at her and murmured something like,

"Enjoying the attention before becoming a housewife?"

Voula was furious. Furious and inventive as she marched to her uncle's butcher shop and ordered exactly 6.7 metres (22 feet) of spoiled animal intestines that he wasn't going to sell. "Make it smelly too," said Voula as she waited for her uncle to stuff the goods on a rusty hand trolley that she would later pull through the streets of Athens and into the professor's office.

When she entered the empty building in the afternoon, exasperated by the smell and the push-back of the trolley, Voula decided that dropping the intestines on the professor's rug wasn't going be enough. She borrowed a surgical scalpel from the lab and decided to show him how long and how wide the human gut could be.

The smell was nasty, the books and the furniture were ruined, but Voula had shown that smug ass (pun intended) what she was capable of. When the professor entered the lab in the following morning, screaming about the little savage who had thrown the ugly slime all around his academic regalia, also looking very slimy himself as he had slipped and slid through the butcher's finely selected concoctions, he barked, "I will find that little boy who thinks he's a man and I will show him who the real man is."

Voula was furious again. She was being unnoticed for the second time around, but when my grandma caught her forehead pumping, she took her hand and held her down until the professor had left to take a shower where they washed the pigs before they sliced them open for surgical practice. The professor may have been ignorant about this housewife's rage, but her classmates weren't, as they turned around to stare at the slicer and to give her a warm round of applause. No med student ever dared to ask her out after this, and they would call her 'Voula the knife'. Voula found that to be a feministic accolade as she got her degree and married her uncle's colleague at the butcher shop. After all, she never knew when she would need his help.

Just as Voula, gut issues often go unnoticed by medical professionals as people tend to be reluctant to discuss them until, just as Voula, they can no longer be ignored. Irritable bowel syndrome, acid reflux, constipation, bloating, different aches are only some of the tell-signs that something may be off.

The Gastrointestinal (GI) tract is about 25 ft long, and it extends from a person's mouth to their anus. The GI tract includes every part and organ of their digestive system, specifically their mouth, oesophagus, stomach, and intestines[1]. The gut flora otherwise referred to as the gut microbiota, refers to the microorganisms that live in humans' GI tracts.

These microorganisms are bacteria, archaea, and fungi[2].

The gut-brain axis is the sequence of signals between the GI tract and a person's Central Nervous System (CNS) that includes their brain and spinal cord[3]. Signals between the GI tract and the CNS can be triggered by neurological, hormonal, or immune processes in the body. At the same time, dysfunctions that may occur in the gut-brain axis can have pathological effects on the entire body[4].

While the literature on the effects of the CNS on the GI tract is ample, research on the impact of the GI tract on the CNS is a developing field[5]. There is no debate, however, on the notion that the gut-brain axis is bidirectional and that each part is able to affect the other[6]. Crucial in gut-brain communication are the microorganisms that live in and beyond the human GI tract. An estimate of $3x10^{13}$ bacterial cells live in the entirety of the human body[7], creating an ecosystem, otherwise known as the human biome[8]. Research also shows that 95% of our body's serotonin and 50% of its dopamine are produced in the gut[9]. This is why gut dysbiosis (the prevalence of bad over good gut bacteria) can lead to depression and anxiety disorders, among others[10].

Let me simplify this. Do you ever rush to the toilet when you get anxious? This can be a sign that your brain affects your gut. What's new to the party is that we have billions of little creatures living inside and on us and that their interaction really, I mean really, affects our lives. What's also new to the party is the idea that what's going on in your gut also affects your brain. In recent years, scientists have linked mood disorders to nutrient depletion, showcasing that symptoms of both overlap. These symptoms may include fatigue (my favourite), anxiety, depression, irritability, overeating, and sleep disturbances, among others.

Now, if you're suffering from intense anxiety or depression, I understand why the last place you'd want to look at is your gut health. I have been there, and I remember thinking that ice cream is one of my few pick-me-ups and that

I was not willing to give it up, especially when I was spending three days in bed due to exhaustion. But sometimes gut health isn't about what you take out of your diet but mostly about what you add to it, so hold on, sir. We'll get to that.

A gut-health approach to mental illness or to general psychological distress may seem a little woo-woo, but I coined the catchphrase 'hippies will outrun you' a couple of years ago, and I plan on proving it. Scientists who focus on the gut-brain axis attribute psychological symptoms to factors such as gastrointestinal dysfunction, oxidative stress, inflammation, and/or nutritional deficiencies. Little did Voula know, but that bunch of grossness she carried around and spread across that professor's office was actually a pretty powerful organ, able to manage peoples' psychological wellbeing and, as I eventually learned, peoples' neurological health too. Is Voula real? You'll never know.

Chapter 3
Neuropsychologists
Binge at Night

My supervisor at the neuropsychiatric hospital that I mentioned earlier has the built of the blue power ranger, the height of Dora the Explorer, and the hair of a grey Danny DeVito. Every Monday, he would welcome me into the lab and show me the stats of his bike rides across Athens. Most of them were 60km, and he would brag that he was never tired, could keep going for hours, but his wife would get worried.

This supervisor advertised himself as a man abstinent from wine, sugar, and all other mortal vices. He kept mentioning how his wife could not hold back from eating an entire tray of brownies, drinking a whole bottle of Coca-Cola and finishing up a bag of chips while they were watching movies. What a joy, I would think, to be married to the snack IRS!

He was (and still is) a lovely man who kept chastising patients who were chubbier than him (a.k.a. everyone). He kept saying, "Just limit your salt consumption, don't eat sugar, no tasting food while cooking it, no high fat, no this, no that." I always had the impulse to chase these people down the hallway and remind them that a neuropsychologist is not a dietician, yet I needed the job, so I stayed put.

Superman, as I used to think of him, would bring a banana with him every morning, and he would place it on top of his clothe-hanger so that it wouldn't turn black as the day progressed. Seldom did he eat the banana, yet I had seen him drink water now and again. A few months into the externship, and knowing my interest in all things gut and diet-related, the supervisor confided in me. He said that he had been waking up at night and 'attacking' the fridge. Now, attacking is a strong word, especially for someone who I speculated ate two slices of melon per night and then would pray for holy forgiveness until dawn. When he asked me what he should do, I inquired about his food choices throughout the day.

"Some almonds with coffee for breakfast, then fish and salad for lunch and a yoghurt for dinner."

Yikes! I thought. I didn't even use to eat like that during my prime modelling years. I couldn't imagine how his body hadn't protested this earlier.

"You need much more fibre," I said. "At least 30 grams a day."

Now, for someone who weighs his fish fillets and counts the leaves of their salad (no dressing), 30 grams of fibre may be difficult to achieve as it requires adding oats, rice, beans, fruits (yes, the sugary ones too), and a lot of other foods that seem 'heavier' than a clean protein and non-starchy veg plate. A study from Harvard reports that people tend to consume 10 to 15 grams of fibre a day that is almost half of the recommended amount[11].

So yes, dear reader, we are back to discussing poop again! Did you think we were done? The fibre found in all of the foods mentioned above tends to absorb water, and it tends to fill up people's stomachs much faster than foods that lack it. Fibre not only helps us control the portions that we are eating as there is literally less space for more, but it also keeps us full for much longer, thus preventing us from attacking our fridges at night-time. Fibre is also a great help in weight loss as it helps with bowel movements that get rid of toxins[12] (yes, this is poop talk).

Seemingly 'heavier' foods, including starchy vegetables such as potatoes, sweet potatoes, butternut squash, corn, and even foods that include starch such as plain bread, have also been destigmatised when it comes to weight loss. An experiment conducted among college students a few years ago found that freshmen who consumed twelve slices of plain bread per day lost more weight than their classmates who didn't[13]. The logic behind this was that bread took up a lot of space in students' stomachs, not allowing them to consume all the unprocessed foods, sweet and salty snacks that they would have had they not eaten the bread. Another researcher found that bread consumption helps with serotonin that prevents people from making unhealthy food choices[14]. Both of these bread-affirming diets have their own sets of rules, such as limiting fat consumption, nulling out alcohol, and exercising for 30 minutes a day. What's important to keep in mind, however, is that starch can help with weight loss, fibre is your gut's friend, and it is an indispensable part of a healthy diet. To elaborate on gut health and weight loss, I must mention one of my failures. Last summer and after my Nutritional Psychology certification, I decided to enrol in a

Nutritional Therapy degree, parallel to my PhD. I really wanted to get first-hand insight as to what was the therapeutic potential of food and how interventions could be implemented. A few weeks before Christmas break, however, I decided that I was not benefitting from the program in a way that could be useful to me and that as it was presented, the information that I was learning could not be combined with my Psychology degree. So I dropped out.

During my stay at the program, however, I learned a couple of very interesting facts about nutrition. One of them was that peoples' digestive systems were used to consuming food that was found in nature and that this is why a plant-based, whole-food diet is the best choice for gut health[15]. Another one was that food was available in nature in ways that could explain their caloric density. This means that almonds were very difficult to find and that they required arduous work before being ready for consumption. One needed to find an almond tree, cut the crops, break the shell and eat it. This is why the caloric 'reward' of almonds is high[16].

A professor at the program, who was also a dietician, mentioned that clients would come to him, saying that they were missing their favourite foods such as pizza, ice cream, apple pies, and French fries. The professor said that he would have one way of responding to all of these complaints. He would say, "You want pizza? You can have pizza. You want apple pie? You can have an entire apple pie. Do you want ice cream with it? You can have it. French fries too? All right. You can have it all. There is only one condition: Make them yourself."

A wonderful Netflix documentary called 'Cooked', mentioned that cooking is a very natural yet largely neglected pillar of health. It mentioned that capitalistic societies have been trying to feed people whenever they get a chance to do so and that this is why even gas stations now sell food. Come to think of it: How does a gas station selling food make sense? It also described how female business owners in India have begun serving home-cooked meals to employees around their cities, thus safeguarding their health and wellbeing. The takeaway from this is: you can't add too many unnatural, difficult to digest, ingredients in a home-cooked meal. Most of what's in there and most of what you end up eating is food that you know and that you recognise. Gut health heaven!

Chapter 4
Neuropsychologists Shouldn't Make Fun of Their Hungry Wives

Going back to my favourite supervisor and his wife, who couldn't resist eating an entire tray of brownies (same here, sister, same here!), there is a reason why he is happy with just a bite, and she can't stop. The reason is: he is indeed superman (just kidding, hold on). The actual explanation can be found in the sugar-mood axis, as well as in research that shows what happens in regular sugar eaters' brains as compared to those who live ascetic lives of abstinence.

During my Nutritional Psychology certification, we had a professor who kept mentioning that when she was younger, she would hit the fridge two or three times a night and who would describe chocolate as the evil devil. "It messed with my brain," she kept saying as if Hershey's held her hostage in an empty cabin and kept being like, "Surrendah, you powerless creature!" I mean, I have definitely surrendered multiple times, and oh, how I miss sweet chocolate now that I can't find a gluten dairy soy-free one (if you want to send one my way, I'll leave my address at the end. ;)

With terror in her eyes and awe in her words, the professor went on to draw a wavy line on the board and to explain how our blood sugar delivers marching orders to our brains. Dictations from the mothership, she would call them, as she would kick out any grown man who would laugh in class at that point. Now, I must clarify that I think of myself as a semi-serious person, but I am absolutely the one who will laugh at inappropriate times, particularly if a sugar-phobic lecturer is putting on a show. In any case, here's what she said.

Apparently, there are three states of being of all of our blood sugars. The optimal one is a stable blood sugar that can be maintained through eating what's considered boring food, such as oats, etc., or through consuming something fun (something sweet), with something boring, that will prevent the sugar spike from skyrocketing. When we eat something super sweet and delicious, our blood sugar does, in fact, skyrocket, and then insulin is released to drive the sugar back to optimal levels. The trick, however, is that when the sugar spike is too high, more insulin is released, leading our blood sugar to drop far below the optimal levels, creating what we call 'low blood sugar'. To address this drop and subsequent fatigue, we tend to grab something that will spike our blood sugar quickly, such as the lecturer's evil devil. After consuming that, however, insulin drops our levels low again, and then a vicious cycle is created[17].

To be honest, I wouldn't call it that vicious because come on, we all have one life to live, and why not enjoy it while we're here? But the takeaways from this lecture were to either abstain from sugars altogether (NOT going to happen) or to interrupt this rise and drop cycle but eat something boring with or after a dessert. That's all. At least that's all I kept from it.

I know I mentioned my dentist/doctor grandmother earlier, but I haven't talked about her fixation on thinness yet. She is a lovely, dynamic, vibrant woman who is, however, a mean harasser of chubby people that land in her way. All of us included. My grandmother has no reservations or sense of political correctness, and I will give you two examples so that you'll believe me.

When eating at a restaurant, she turned around and saw a huge plate of meats landing in front of an unsuspecting, overweight man's seat. She stood up, looked at the kind gentleman, and said, "Ts, ts, ts."

Now, if you're not Greek, you may not know that "ts, ts, ts" is an expression of disapproval. When the man gayly ignored my grandma and went about his merry way (chewed on the first piece of meat), my grandma cleared her throat and tried again. This time louder. "TS, TS, TSSSSSS," she cried, and when the man finally looked at her, she was ready to sit. He then stood up (because it is his prerogative), came to our table, looked at my grandma, and asked her what she was having for lunch. "A sensible salad," she said, and the man wasted no time before saying,

"A proper cow's meal."

The second event that haunted my childhood and made me apprehensive to go shopping with her was at a department store. My grandma truly is a loving person who will go out of her way to say kind things to people, but she is unyielding in believing that fat is the sole precursor of death and a tell-tale of a sinful life, and she makes sure to share this wisdom with anyone who will and who won't hear it. As I was trying on a

31

shirt that I needed for a school play, a quirky lady marched outside of her dressing room, made a swirl in front of my grandma (I know, we should be warning people), and asked her if she liked the jacket she had on. "It has a fighting character," said my grandma, and I breathed again as I had suspected what could come of this.

"It fits like a glove," said the lady, and then my grandma cleared her throat again (at which point I wanted to scream to the lady: RUN, run while you still have time), and she said,

"It has a fighting character because it is putting on a fight to stay put. It's very small. You can lose the weight and then it will be perfect."

My grandmother may have said that she never ate sugar in her life, but my siblings and I know for a fact that wasn't true. Every time she would pick us up from school (that was every Tuesday), she would open our bags, find our sweet snacks that Mom had given us (usually cookies or a chocolate bar), and would wolf them down before the engine was warm enough to drive. If we had fruit juices, she would take these too as she always forgot to eat and then would come to us starving and impatient.

My grandmother's favourite saying is "I won't eat ANYTHING" whenever we are about to sit down and have a family meal. My uncle will offer to serve her food, and she will reiterate, "I won't eat. Who needs all this food? Do you know how unhealthy it all is?"

Of course, she will end up eating the most among all of us, still pretending that she ate nothing. The trick, however, is that you should never acknowledge that she actually did consume a crumb because you may be risking her eating nothing for a week to cleanse herself.

One of her best ideas (the greatest, however, will be presented in the next chapter), came when she heard that people who have more body fat than others tend not to be able to stop craving sugary foods after consuming just a little sugar. People of normal body fat percentages, however, do tend to be able to stop after a bite, just like my supervisor.

"George!" she said to my uncle. "I know what you'll do! You will lose a lot of weight, and then you won't crave food anymore!" We then hid her in the house so that NASA wouldn't poach her and take her with them.

Chapter 5
Please Give Me a Skinny Person's Poo!

My grandmother's food aversion and respective fat-phobic crusades have landed most of us (and unfortunately other people too) to therapists' offices who have tried to convey the importance of food as fuel that is NECESSARY (how surprising) for the survival of humans and all other life on the planet. From all of us, our uncle, who lives in the same building as my grandmother, has received her greatest ideas about weight loss.

Now, weight loss is not my grandma's only source of inspiration. She is a very successful woman and wants the same for her children and grandchildren, so whenever she encounters a success story, she calls one of us (we are nine) and explains what the game plan is. I have always been expecting her to meet a prima ballerina, call me and say, "I bought you pointes, start stretching, see you in 10."

I love this woman more than life itself, and we actually share a pace of thinking that is quite unarresting, unsettling, and incomprehensible to most. If I call her at 6 AM to tell her I have decided to try out for another Masters in

Gastroenterology that I hope to get accepted in as a neuropsychologist in training although I have no pure medical background, she'll say, "Go for it," without mentioning how crazy the idea sounds.

This is why, when I read about faecal microbiota transplants in relation to weight loss, I had a hunch I shouldn't share this information with her. Does the word faecal ring a bell? Well, it should because it comes from faeces (yikes, I know). The procedure involves transferring processed, liquid stools with healthy bacteria into the intestines of a receiver. Some studies have found that people of normal weight who received overweight peoples poos, became overweight themselves[18]. Others found that overweight poo receivers whose donors were of normal weight, actually lost weight[19]. All this can be explained by the functions of the microbiome and its effects on the body[20]. Knowing how crazy this may sound, I did have a reservation about sharing it with my grandma. But when she asked about how my research was going, I couldn't resist.

"George!" she promptly cried to my uncle. "Come down! We're getting you a dose of skinny poo!"

Chapter 6
Expedition 30 Plants a Week

"Theeertey," cried my German camping love interest. "Theeertey iss a vehghan's meagic nouumbah," he went on. Little did I know at the time, but the man was referring to a 30x30 rule that has taken over gut-health rules over the past few years. 30 grams of fibre a day[12], 30 different plants a week for diversity and optimal function.[21] Plants include vegetables, rice, nuts, seeds, fruits, beans, and many, many things that make up a good shower-free, smelly road trip with a farty blonde vegan that I met a couple of weeks ago on a Greek beach near our summer house. By the way, a cook from India eventually suggested mustard seeds for gas. They do the trick!

Albert had landed in Greece with a tiny red backpack and a receipt for a camping car rental that he wanted to drive around Peloponnese until August. We bonded over our love for 'Expedition Happiness', a German documentary of a couple that flew to New York, bought a school bus, converted it into a luxury house on wheels, and drove from Alaska to Mexico City, in pursuit of an unconventional lifestyle, along with their dog Rudy. The girl's name was Mogli, she is a wonderful singer that you should look up, and Albert told me

I reminded him of her given my brown eyes and tan skin. What a rare resemblance, I know!

Off we went to the rural roads of Southern Greece, as I began to learn more and more about the friendly tourist who had just heard a podcast with Tim Spector, a British epidemiologist, who claimed that 30 plants a week are what we need for a healthy microbiome. Excited as I was about the gut, I decided to join Albert in taking on the 30-a-week challenge, and I tried to google the schedules of farmer's markets around the peninsula. Turns out, the road trip was actually a scavenger hunt for fresh produce as Albert was passionate about eating food that was definitely organic. When we sat down at a fast-food restaurant that, surprisingly offered salmon fillets, he asked the waiter where they came from and if they were killed in an ethical manner. The poor man looked at him, brows lift to the sky, shoulders shrugged, and said, "A big car brings them over."

When we got to Mani, a small town of historical significance, we got into a negotiation with a pair of Scottish brothers, 30 and 32 years old, who were about to buy the last available courgettes to fry chips with, outside of their illegally set camping tent. Courgettes were the only thing they bought, and as we figured out later when they invited us over for dinner (that's how we resolved the negotiation), they survived on tinned tomatoes, canned beans, canned coconut milk, and some herbs that were gifted to them by an old lady in Nafplion. Mathew and Zach, these were their names, explained that they too were vegan, yet they were on a mission to democratise vegan food by creating one pound recipes for university students and anyone living on a budget. They explained that the difference between canned and organic isn't that grave, and if one were to choose between canned veggies and beans, or a processed snack, they'd rather he or she chose the cans.

These brothers were a godsent as they not only convinced Albert to try the tins, but they also joined the road trip for three days and decided to teach us a couple of tricks and recipes on the go. Matt said that when he first turned vegan, he felt like hc would only be able to eat grated carrots and celery, yet he then figured out that a healthy lifestyle can be achieved by focusing more on what you add than on what you take out of your diet. He, too, pursued the 10-a-day, 30-a-week rule for consuming different plants, and he achieved that by adding combinations of seeds, herbs, and multicoloured beans and lentils here and there.

For my sweet tooth that was missing summer ice creams and refreshing desserts, he suggested freezing grapes, whisking cold bananas with some almond milk and cinnamon, or even rolling dates on raw cacao. On dates, I drew the line as they had been reminding me of cockroaches for YEARS before anyone said I should try them. When he skinned and pitted them, though, they were, in fact, tasty.

If you are a student on a budget or want to try a variety of plants to meet the 30 per week rule, here are two one-pound recipes Matt and Zach taught us. Just kidding. Google one-pound vegan recipes and anything you find will be better than what I've retained. Plus, were you really going to use a book with the word 'shits' in its title as a recipe source? Come on!

Chapter 7
Congressional Fellowship

Neuropsychology may be my chosen profession but being a scatter-mind is my lifelong vocation. Just as my grandma, I never let a good idea pass me by without giving it a try. So far, I have been: a content creator for Bacardi, a marketing intern for Korres, a retail operations' intern for Salvatore Ferragamo, a HuffPost blogger, a retail operations' assistant for Guess, a Thrive Global blogger, a fashion model, a therapist, a published fiction writer, and a neuropsychologist in training. My mind does travel vast surfaces in minimal amounts of time, and I never want to regret not attempting something. This is why the list goes on. So far, I have dropped out of: dental school, drama school, business school, and I have yet to try law school.

Last year, however, and during the first covid quarantine, I decided that psychology wasn't enough to help me advocate for social issues that I was passionate about, and I wondered whether pursuing a dual degree, a J.D. along with my PhD, would be worth it. My brother, who is already a lawyer, tried to dissuade me from pursuing that, too, especially after I started receiving positive feedback from law schools. I may be a scattered mind, but I'm a lucky one too because I do work hard and because my woo-woo approach to creativity keeps telling me: there is a reason why you had this hunch, so you better persevere until you grant yourself an opportunity here.

People often assume that I'm unfocused when I mention my versatile resume, but you better know I am hyper-focused, and I also love cross-pollinating every field that will have me with lessons from all the others. Fiction writing, for example, helped me author a cover letter for a fellowship that would cover all of my remaining PhD tuition and some living expenses in a convincing way. The award was a research-based grant, and the bank that was handling the money of a rich heiress wanted to know what my dissertation was about.

About an hour before meeting with the awards coordinator of my school, I had watched the 'Fed Up' documentary with Katie Couric. The documentary was fascinating, and it was explaining how advertising, processed food availability, and lack of information lead underprivileged parts of the U.S. to suffer from obesity, having their children develop metabolic diseases from very young ages too. It also takes on Michelle Obama's 'Let's Move' campaign, which ended up having the adverse effects of what it originally intended while also leading people back to processed food choices.

Trustful as I am towards my hunches and divine timing, I decided to present a dissertation idea to the awards coordinator that was very close to what I had just watched. A quick google search depicted an overlap of underprivileged parts of the U.S., such as some parts of Florida and Texas, where Alzheimer's and Parkinson's are most prevalent, and where food choices seem to be the most unhealthy across the States.

In my first nutritional therapy class, I had learned about food deserts that aren't areas in which food is not available. They are actually areas in which natural, unprocessed food such as fruit and vegetables are not at all available, and all people can consume are ultra-processed snacks and meals that are often advertised as healthy[22]. Another important thing that I learned is that in areas like these, in which children have been brought up without having tried unprocessed produce, yet having been used to eating foods that are tailored to be hyper-exciting taste-wise when presented with a simple strawberry, their taste pallets cannot recognise the sweetness of it as they have been dulled by made up ingredients[23]. Food deserts are exactly what the 'Fed Up' documentary was taking on.

My neuropsych background at the time made me consider all the research that I had read about neurodegenerative disorders, including Alzheimer's and Parkinson's being linked to gut dysbiosis, which is a prevalence of 'bad' bacteria in one's gut due to poor diet, stress, and many other factors linked to a low socioeconomic status[24,25].

My research hypothesis was dual. First, I needed to confirm that there was a correlation between the prevalence of these neurodegenerative disorders and unhealthy life choices in these areas. Second, I needed to explore why these peoples' diets were unhealthy.

Was it a lack of availability? Lack of health education? Misinformation from the media? Beliefs about healthy food being expensive (Many have said that lentils, for example, used to be peasant food. Also taking into consideration Matt's and Zach's love for canned goods, this may be a misconception)? Beliefs about unprocessed food being untasty (remember the taste pallet insight and children's inability to identify strawberries as sweet)? Was it beliefs about healthy food taking longer to prepare (okay, this one is true, but you can have pretty good dahl in 20')?

The awards coordinator, who turned out to be an advocate for healthy food herself, really applauded the idea and then told me to put together a five-year plan to present to the board that would give out the grant. I went to bed that night furious about what I had seen in the documentary, sad for all of the children who presented themselves, claimed to be willing to put in the effort to lose weight (remember, they were obese), trying, losing some of it, only to gain it back a few months after the documentary was filmed. This was a good instance, I thought, of when a law degree would be useful for advocacy.

I read an article once that said that in the early hours of the day, the human brain is hyperactive and hyper-associative, and I find this to be very true. The morning after my documentary viewing and meeting with the coordinator, I woke up brainstorming ideas for advocacy. I wanted to learn if psychologists could in any way impact public policy, I googled it, and I found out about the American Psychological Association's Congressional Fellowship at Capitol Hill. Every year, licensed psychologists with 2+ years of experience were welcomed in the team of a member of Congress and were advising them (not sure to what extent) on psychology or neuropsychology-related matters.

If you've watched My Big Fat Greek Wedding, you will know that Mr Portokalos would end most of his sentences with "there you go!", when these were aimed at solving a problem. As I needed a five-year plan for my grant application, I pulled out my notepad and wrote. "Next year –

PhD. & neuropsych externship. Then: neuropsych internship and graduation. Then: 1-year neuropsych postdoc and psychology license exam. Then: 2nd-year neuropsych postdoc and neuropsych license exam. Then: Congressional Fellowship. There you go."

This five-year plan may seem quite specific or even too ambitious, ego-boosting, and semi-narcissistic to some (or all of you benevolent, kind-hearted readers), but there is no harm in trying. Or, if you are my brother George who has studied government, history, and then law at Georgetown University and who is destined to enter politics whether he likes it or not, there is indeed harm in trying as I've officially become his number one stalker who shows up wherever he goes. "When are you planning on applying for the Capitol Hill spot?" asked my mom when I shared my plans with her (big mistake). Greek moms have one way of responding to ambitious plans, and this is by saying: "From this side, you should sleep," (με αυτό το πλευρό να κοιμάσαι), which means, ain't gonna happen loser.

"When are you planning on applying for the Congressional Fellowship?" she asked again.

"Whenever George is ready to move back to D.C.," I responded.

Chapter 8
Making It Cool

I went to a posh private school in Greece that required us to wear uniforms all through elementary school until we progressed to Juicy Couture velour tracksuits and Abercrombie tanks from seventh grade and beyond. Uniforms thus persistent until Commencement (our high school graduation), while we were not allowed to wear 'hot shorts', as the vice principal used to call them, have extra piercings (on our faces at least), or 'crazy hair' (this one was coined by the principle).

There were slight deviations in our personal styles, some would choose low-cut Converse shoes while others would prefer Nike's millennials, yet no one really stood out. With one exception. A girl with who I used to have dance classes, in third grade, whose real name I can't recall, and who used to bring squishy eyeballs that she had filled with her 'family's blood' after they had had it drawn for cholesterol exams. I know this is too detailed a description, but when I went to my non-doctor grandma to ask if I could have our own family's blood after the lab had analysed it, she performed a mini exorcism with olive oil and some feta cheese.

This girl used to be blonde until high school, when she revolted, died it purple, drew large chunks of circles around her eyes, wore hippie clothes (the same ones each day), and sat on the central building's stairs holding a backpack that wrote "THE STOMACH". Although I wasn't much of a hippie myself around then (I had sworn not to wear Juicy pants – Abercrombie tops were enough), I definitely admired her determination to stand against the institution's fashion, perhaps its values too.

I don't know why, but I assumed at the time that the girl was vegan. Something about her showed that she respected animals more than she did humans and that she probably preferred them as a company too. Before getting diagnosed with celiac and a myriad food intolerances (okay, okay, they are just two), I was very minimalistic when it came to food.

That does not mean that I ate minimal portions but that I liked to keep things simple and repetitive. To be candid, I could eat the exact same ice cream cone for breakfast, lunch, and dinner, and then repeat for six months until something new came along. I was the queen of monophagia (eating one thing again and again), and I had also developed a travellers' approach to food choices.

I am someone who has voyaged across Europe, the US, Asia, and Africa, and this experience comes with non-existent expectancies about home-cooked meals. Snacks were my main source of subsistence, and I loved buying all my meals from the same kiosks or tiny supermarkets every morning, no matter where I was. Pre-packaged food brought me great joy, and I remember tearing the fragile wraps of tasty goodness at different times, in different life stages.

I have fond memories of Oreo bubble Milka's in Cape Town, weird tasting Sneakers in Mexico, Jell-O instant pudding in London, and Algida ice creams in Lisbon and Sorrento. My go-to in Greece were Delta chocolate cones, the largest ones that actually had fewer calories than the smaller Magnum ones. Hungry? Same here. I am also not so proud to say that I have tasted diet-coke in Greece, France, Italy, Germany, Austria, Spain, Portugal, Morocco, Johannesburg, Singapore, and the US, and they all taste different. The worst by far is the US one (although it comes in larger bottles), and the best is the English one, in my humble opinion. Ahh, how I miss the trashy goodness. What I mean to say by all this is that when I was first diagnosed, I had to give up A LOT. My entire diet had to change as nothing was dairy, gluten, and soy-free.

The universe works in mysterious ways, as, when I was visiting my brother in New York about five years ago, I was experiencing intense anxiety and had decided to research natural ways of addressing it. In the basement of Strand Books, an infamous bookstore near Manhattan's Union Square, I found a book that discussed tackling one's anxiety through dietary interventions.

I skimmed through the pages with one hand, wolfing down Skinny Pop popcorn with the other, and read that I should give up on dairy, gluten, soy, and sugar. HA! I said and threw the poor thing out the window (literally. I then had to walk down and get it because local patrols would hand out tickets like chewing gum). Little did I know at the time that I would eventually have to give up on all of this except one – sweet, sweet sugar.

I know that there is a large conversation around whether we should or shouldn't consume sugar, how honey and other sources are healthier, all the skin, body, and soul benefits of quitting it cold turkey, but this is my only thing that's left. I do eat honey, but I'll definitely not shy away from the real thing if we cross pathways.

During my first weeks in this new diet, I was eating fish, really bad omelettes, some almonds, fruit, and lots and lots of grated carrots (just like Matt from the road trip).

Everything tasted like cardboard, and as I was getting used to it, I watched the What the Health documentary on Netflix and decided to abstain from even more and go full-blown vegan.

In the midst of this transition, YouTube was a lifesaver as it helped me learn the basics about tofu (can't have it as it's soy-based), tempeh (can't have it either), and lentils as a protein base (this I can have). These little videos created a sense of a fictitious yet welcoming community that would support me through my ugly-tasting cooking endeavours. Through them, I not only learned about super (okay, not thaaaat super but good enough) tasting recipes, but I also heard about tricks that would help me in my very green journey.

One of the main tips that I heard was to build a real community or to at least find one more person who is interested in the food that you are interested in so that you can motivate each other. At the time, I had exactly zero vegan, vegetarian, or even plant-based friends, and I had zero ones willing to try anything I would make either. This would be a good time to reach out to "THE STOMACH", I thought, but

I then remembered that I hadn't actually heard that she was vegan. She just fit the part.

In thinking about food, especially when we were still in school (pre-university), I remember fitness being celebrated, I remember thinness being celebrated, but I clearly remember healthy food being despised. There was only one mom at school who had dared to serve ginger coke and date-based desserts at their daughter's first party and let me just say, there was never a second one.

My brother and I spent some time discussing how we'd like to nurture our hypothetical children (if we ever have any) in relation to food as we were walking home from the Empire Diner on 9th Avenue one night. Our grandmother's "I won't let your jeans tighten" crusade has clearly left all of us body-conscious and anxious when it comes to food, so we are adamant about ending this cycle within this family generation.

After years of contemplation, I think that my game plan is the following: Eat everything (that I can – there's kind of a lot excluded already) whenever I'm hungry, desert too, show how fun exercise can be, play active games and never, EVER say I want to lose weight, I am dissatisfied with my body, I wish I was thinner, or comment on other peoples' bodies as children are sponges and they definitely will grasp that and run with it. To practice for the game plan, I'm already doing all this.

As previously explained, a gut-healthy diet is one that includes a large variety of foods. It is a nutrient-dense one, and it is refreshing in that it is, in fact, not about what you take out but about all that you can add-in. Whenever I share this with friends, they seem to be reluctant to add to their plates as they find that it will lead to weight gain. Nutrient-dense diets are not weight-loss or weight-gain plans. They are health-promoting diets, and for some reason, people seem to be perplexed by that.

Come to think of it, we are so cautious about eating more or more of something, even if it's health-promoting, but when it comes to popular elimination diets, we do no challenging. Here is a list of what's cool and what's not, based on my estimation of popular opinion (which may, of course, be invalid):

For weight loss:

- Dukan diet: okay
- Atkins diet: okay
- Keto diet: okay
- Paleo diet: okay
- (Mostly) for ethical reasons:
- Vegan diet: okay
- Vegetarian diet: okay
- Pescatarian diet (they may not like fish – let them be): somewhat okay

For healthy ageing:

- Nutrient-dense diet: ABSURDITY!

Chapter 9
Art of the Bloat

I used to get somewhat disoriented whenever I would gain some and then lose some weight, until I realised that certain peoples' faces would absolutely light up whenever they saw me fuller than before. I'm not talking about a family member who was concerned about me being too thin, but I'm referring to a couple of randos, who I may have exchanged one word with prior to that, and who would merrily walk up to me and say, "Did you get fat?"

Happier than a kid on Christmas morning.

As many people who have gastrointestinal problems or autoimmune conditions, I have definitely lived in different body types in one lifetime. Tallness really is the only constant. Until I'm 70, that's when I'll really plunge as my great aunt Loula used to say (yes, Greek female names do sound the same). As I've heard the randos describe me, I have been from normal, to thin-normal, to skinny, to semi-anorexic, to normal again, and the cycle is ever-revolving. Although I have pretty much always been comfortable within a body type, I haven't been that comfortable being in transition from one body type to another. What I mean to say is, I'm okay with being normal when six months ago I was super skinny but I don't like getting there because of two main reasons.

The first is that celiac driven bloating feels like someone literally blew air across my front side, from my throat to my feet. This is usually making me feel like one of these blow-up balloons that can't bend over when kids pull it down at parties. I may not look it, but I certainly feel it. The second is that people will either make celebratory or derogatory comments about it, while it's already difficult to move around feeling like a blow-up. The transitions from one body type to another are the times when I'm least confident because not all clothes fit me the same, I find it difficult to move at times, and I'm not sure where I'll land. This is making me feel awkward and not so sexy (yes, all women are allowed to want to feel sexy).

In any case, when I've landed in a body type, I am usually confident again and that is when comments such as 'did you get fat' make me wonder about why it's such a sensitive topic for women, why women are usually the ones to make such comments, and why having weights that change feels wrong. After my celiac diagnosis, I have been more or less stable but there are definitely times when my symptoms flare up and I go through this song and dance again.

I was listening to a Greek stand-up comedy show in which the comedian (a woman) asked the women in the audience who were happy with their bodies to clap. Two people clapped, the comedian looked over and said "Okay, one's my brother, and the other is the camerawoman who's trying to create a wave." She then said that she had asked of several audiences and whenever there was a singular woman who clapped, others would turn around to look at her and would murmur: "Mmmmm, not that great bitch."

I know that it's a pop culture saying that maintaining a healthy weight is good, but I have truly never been someone with a stable body type and I don't think that I ever will. It doesn't matter how much I exercise or if I really pay attention to what I eat, if my gut wants me to be bloated, I will be bloated and that is that. Sometime in my early twenties, I grew obsessed with weighting myself every morning, noticing and keeping track of the slightest changes. I also saw on a documentary that Ernest Hemingway did the same at his home in Cuba, where he would take note of the number on his wall. I didn't share Hemingway's habit, nor any of his literary talents, let's be honest, but I did spend a lot of mental energy on this (I then addressed it in therapy, thank you very much). During my time as a weight-obsessed youngster, I noticed a couple of things that I'd like to share with you:

1. Even the slightest weight gain could ruin my day and make me feel like I was off to a wrong start. This negative feeling would carry until the end of the day and then the next morning until the next weigh-in.

2. If five minutes before I checked my weight in the morning, I felt like I had gained, my mood would drop, I would definitely feel like a failure and then if I stepped on the scale and realised I was actually the same or less, I would feel so, so much better about myself and my worth. That shit's fucked up.

3. Weighting myself so much was not only self-policing but also a type of apology for being a normal human who may not know how to or may not be able to manage this fucking number.

4. If I had gained weight in my morning check-in, I would NOT be motivated to work out, go do fun things or enjoy a good meal. I may have eventually done all these things, but not in a good mood.

5. The main thing that made me feel better was witnessing beautiful women of versatile body types be confident, do their jobs and have fun, without seeming (at least on the outside), like their self-consciousness was holding them back.

6. Another thing that made me feel better was realising that first, I'm not as young as I once used to be and I will not be self-policing for the rest of my life and second, there is a difference between not liking the body type that I'll land in and not like the transition and the resulting feeling of bloating that is also linked to gastrointestinal challenges. I do like what I look like, all of what I look like, and (not but), I do find it challenging sometimes to stay positive during a symptom flare.

7. Symptom flares are also linked to the menstrual cycle and what it means to be a woman whose body is working, sometimes retaining more water than others. I do want to have kids one day, even if that means that my weight will vary drastically from one week to another because I am a woman, and because I need to actively look after my gut health given my background.

8. Making friends who have had their own health challenges that had and still have an impact on their body, really, REALLY helps put things in

perspective. Also opening up conversations like these can be healing in its own little way.

9. Last and most important thing. Our bodies may be changing, we may look different twice or thrice a year but guess what. WE ARE ALLOWED. Successful men and women who are interesting, who live full lives, who have a great impact on the world, or who have smaller, kinder impacts and lead simple, beautiful lives, come in all, and I mean ALL shapes and sizes. These shapes and sizes can also change within the very same person. They are allowed. Self-policing one's weight is not only a way of apologising for one's body but also of being conditionally free. We should be free through all our changing messiness.

Chapter 10
Ear Farts at Work

An upside to staying in Greece due to covid is getting to swim and do water sports further into fall than usual. A downside to that is getting ear infections because you underestimated the wind's effect on your drums. Mine at least got ruptured last year, leading me to a doctor who suggested closing my nose with my fingers and then blowing until all medicine has exited the hole (yikes, I know). As the doctor did not warn me to stop doing that after I had left his office, leaving my ear unable to heal for a while, I continued to blow out my ears a few times a day, sometimes at work too.

I could hear the wheezing noise of the blowout, but of course, I would – it was literally in my ear. This technique offered me great relief as I had been feeling a weight in my ear; apparently, that is what happens when you can't hear really well from one side. That is why, when I was having trouble hearing people at work, I would discretely grab my nose over my covid facemask and blow as hard as I could (not recommended – it may bring you some relief, but it will also give you covid that will cause you death). Come to think of it, this technique did absolutely nothing to restore my hearing that was caused by the rupture, but I kept at it like an explorer digging for gold.

This went on for about two weeks until I had a day off, stayed at home with my mom, and had the urge to repeat the blowout. I grabbed my nose, blew hard, and my mom rolled down the floor laughing about the SOUND that this made. "Oh my God, can you hear it?" I said. "Can I hear it? Can you not?" I could, but I thought that was because it was IN my literal ear hole.

"That's okay," she said to appease my emerging embarrassment about having had this happen at work, "they'll think it's your celiac acting up."

Besides the entertainment of my colleagues, this infection led me to a two-week antibiotic treatment, as the damn infection wouldn't subside (blowing may have had something to do with that). I come from a medical family, and this means that I do not take antibiotics unless something is life-threatening and I'm on my last leg. Having gotten the green light to take them, however, I didn't think twice of it until the round was done, and I had bloating, and gut pain like you wouldn't believe. People do say, take probiotics with antibiotics, but Greeks actually have an expression that goes "we have steady stomachs" (έχουμε γερό στομάχι), so we take the prescription as a light suggestion. "Nah," we say until we're bent in half and have difficulty breathing.

Two weeks of heavy antibiotics can really do a number on you (a number two, to be specific). To soothe my gut health that was greatly adrift, I googled post-treatment remedies and found nothing. Everything was just about what you can do during the treatment. In any case, I decided the probiotics were the way to go, so I ordered some online, took them for a month, and absolutely nothing happened. After this was done, I was watching some

Instagram stories of a nutritionist who mentioned that not all probiotics are the same.

After I went to the pharmacy to inquire about which probiotics are best for post-antibiotic rounds, they gave me a similar response to the one Albert had received about the salmon fillets in the fast-food restaurant: "They just bring them in boxes." Upset and disoriented, I decided to wing it. I had a friend once who tried to make their own yoghurt, bought probiotics, and gave us all diarrhoea, and I remembered they had used some neon green ones (the box was neon green – had the pills been that the diarrhoea was not that surprising). I saw the green box amidst the wilderness, picked it up, bought it, and hoped for the best.

Just as with my gluten, dairy, life-free diet, two days in the probiotics, my pain had vanished, and I felt much lighter. I have been taking them ever since. Now, because apparently, it's true that all probiotics are not the same, and because I find the information that is written on them greatly unintelligible, all I can say is, probiotics are a good way to boost your gut health as they add good bacteria in your microbiome, but I cannot be the one to tell you which ones to choose or why. Ask your pharmacist, and if they don't know, I'll be happy to snap a pic of my neon ones (just kidding – don't want to get in trouble).

Breaking the Gas Ceiling

Chapter 11
Gut-Related Inventions I
Never Carried to Fruition

When I was 21 years old and living in Los Angeles, working for a fashion brand that I was largely disinterested in, I was urged by a loved one to apply for an MBA in Boston. A few months later, I had gotten in with a full scholarship, and fast forward to a year later, I had turned the offer down and was modelling to pay for Psych studies. My ingenious business talent, however, was not wasted, as I keep having ground-breaking ideas that will revolutionise gut-brain health in the years to come. To attest to my brainstorming abilities, here are a few of the products that I have thought of creating (and hey, perhaps one day I will):

- **A portable toilet kit including a white noise machine and a deodorant lavender spray for IBS.** White noise machines are a therapist's best friend as you turn them on before entering a room, and no one can hear what is happening in that room until you turn them back off again. Lavender bathroom sprays are a US invention (I haven't seen them anywhere in

Europe), and I think they are genius. About a lifetime ago, I was working as an intern at the corporate offices of Salvatore Ferragamo on Fifth Avenue, and I remember seeing these sprays waiting there, beside the luxurious toilets, and not knowing what they were. Five years later, I was vising my brother and his husband in their apartment in New Jersey, and I saw one of these there too. I asked about them, and George (my brother) explained what they were all about. How convenient, I thought. During my first year as a PhD student in NY, I was suffering from the side effects of celiac that was then misdiagnosed as Irritable Bowel Syndrome. I had missed quite a few classes because of it, and I remembered thinking that the paper-thin walls between the bathroom stalls weren't making my life any easier. I definitely found the white noise – lavender deodorant idea genius – and I googled how to go about making it. What I came up with were leasing products to create gift baskets (not exactly what I was going for). There was also the conundrum of where to place the white noise machine or how to gradually build the sound up so that people wouldn't realise that someone had just entered a stall and a giant wave sound emersed from the toilet seat.

- **Multivitamins for depression and different ones for anxiety.** As I mention elsewhere in the book, depression has been linked to deficiencies in B Vitamins, Omega 3 fatty acids, iron, selenium, iodine, tryptophan, magnesium, vitamin D, and zing, while anxiety has been linked to deficiencies in B vitamins, vitamin C and E, magnesium, essential fatty acids, and other minerals. Being the unsuccessful businesswoman that I am, I had an aha moment of "this is a great opportunity to create multivitamins to help with depression and anxiety". After checking with all of the laws regarding whether I could create and run a business while being a psychologist in the US (at least an aspiring one as we officially get licensed after the completion of the PhD), I decided to poach my twin brother, who is a pharmacist. After an icebreaker question, asking him whether they learned how to create medications at university, to which he rolled his eyes upward and then backward towards his deeper thoughts, he told me that creating a multivitamin is pretty simple, that it includes a capsule and other things I haven't kept in my memory. I had found a PMS cherry-based supplement created by two siblings who actually had zero pharmaceuticals' experience and who used to be graphic designers in California. I presented their business model to Jason (my twin), and he said that these gummies were actually super easy to make. "Great," I said. "So you can help me."

"I can, but I don't want to," he responded, and that was the end of my short-lived career in pharmaceuticals.

- **A math formula for a whole-food, plant-based recipe.** My Instagram feed is overflowing with wonderful, tasty, mouth-watering vegan, gluten-free foods created by the world's most creative and innovative amateur and esteemed chefs out there. I, however, have zero instinct for cooking delicious food, and even though I consider myself creative, my juices dry when it comes to making something edible. I do, however, enjoy watching myriads of cooking videos on YouTube, especially during the warm summer days after I've swum in the sea after I've had lunch and while everyone around me is sleeping. Last summer, after watching excited, youthful, and lively chefs create wonderful dahls, stews, cakes, and juices, I decided that I had had enough of complex guidelines, enough of unintelligible hippie cupboard stashes, enough intimidation for one lifetime, and I was going to solve this puzzle forever. I was going to create a formula for a recipe in which most vegetables, beans, rice would work that would give people a central guideline that they could build up from. Efficiency over complexity was my motto, and I went about creating dahl in three different ways to start with. Now I must say that when a family friend asked my mom whether her own mom had taught her how to cook, she said no, she got offended, and she made a list of all of the other important life lessons that her mother had given her, such as to work, to be financially independent, to respect people, to raise good citizens of the world, and so forth. The friend then went about to eat the defrosted cheese pie that Mom had bought for him from the supermarket and realised that there wasn't much food homemaking around. My dahl formula was less diversifiable than my mom's life skills, and I ended up making three identical dishes that I then frosted and ate for the month of August.

- **A Weight-Watchers' type community for healthy eaters.** A benefit of celiac-induced, year-round hibernation is that you get to follow people who you truly admire on the internet.

One of these people is Oprah Winfrey, and another is Gayle King. A three-hour cyber stalk of Gayle King after seeing how she handled an interview with R Kelly led me to her Instagram and to super happy posts about her weight loss journey, sponsored or supported by WW, formerly known as Weight Watchers. An ad for a free seven-day trial of their new app led me to download it and finally realise how the point system worked. I found it very smart indeed, and I also admired the community of people sharing their personal stories and progress, as well as their struggles through a social media-like page that was a part of the app. Never in my life had I witnessed a place more supportive and encouraging than the WW social page that made me consider the possibility of cancelling all other platform accounts and just logging in to this one for positivity. As I wasn't in a weight-loss mood, I realised that tracking food was helping me get an understanding of the diversity of plants and the amount of fibre I was consuming on a daily basis. 10-a-day, 30-a-week plants and 30 grams of fibre were suddenly much easier to track and pursue, all whilst getting the support of beautiful 'friends' from Nebraska to San Diego and from Province to Madrid. How easier, I thought, would my initial switch to a gluten, dairy, soy-free diet be, with the support of all these wonderful people? Perhaps I should create something like this just for healthy eaters, disinterested in weight management. I did not see it through.

- **Healthy diet coke.** This may have nothing to do with the gut-brain axis, but diet coke (or, in EU terms: Coca-Cola light, light cola, and all other names of this heavenly drink) is my central obsession in life. I used to have it from morning to night, for breakfast, lunch, and dinner. I tried replacing it with coffee (eww), tried creating a similar drink with sparkling water, some caffeine, some stevia (and a little throw up at the end), tried getting hooked on ice tea instead, but NOTHING ever gave me the same pleasure and bubbly sense in my mouth. It was love. Whoever makes a healthy diet coke that I can shamelessly drink in litters, I will run away with you. Right now. Email me. ;)

- **Something, anything that would resolve celiac disease.** Okay, this one's my dad's. He got tired after the healthy diet coke idea, gave up, and started shouting, "Just find a damn thing that solves celiac. Okay? No more BS. Eat a sandwich and get a real job!" hands flailing in the air and all. He then left the room.

Chapter 12
Faking It Till I Make It

There is a funny tendency I have noticed amongst women (not all of them, of course) when one achieves a goal and the others didn't think she could or deserved to do it. I do consider myself a feminist, but I also acknowledge that not every woman jumps up to congratulate another when they succeed.

When I completed my internship at the corporate offices of Salvatore Ferragamo in New York at age 20, and then flew back to Greece to finish my Bachelor's degree, I kept hearing people thinking out loud about "What I had to do to get the job?" I spent endless nights dreaming that I would respond with what Erin Brockovich had said to that posh lawyer who couldn't believe she had collected that many signatures in a minimal amount of time. I will bypass the first part of her response because children may be reading this but let's just say that the second part was "my knees are killing me".

Thankfully when I was younger, I was more reserved, so I never got to play this out in real life, but when I first got great neuropsych placements in Greece, I did have a woman dm me on Instagram and literally say, "Who did you have to sleep with to get these jobs?" Little did she know, I was waiting for an opportunity to clap back at haters for more than half a decade, and so I wasted no time and wrote back, "You're overestimating my abilities, I'm not that good in bed."

My transition from general psychology to neuropsychology, mediated by a turn to the gut-brain axis, was serendipitous and quite fast. This made me face a little bit of impostor syndrome, although I worked tirelessly to learn the assessments, the scoring, the report writing, the diagnoses, and the intricacies of their manifestations on each patient. I do believe that I have worked very, very hard to grant myself the opportunities that I have to this day, and I really needed to be strategic about opening more doors in order to eventually be able to do the research and the clinical work that I was passionate about.

When it was time to apply for my second round of neuropsych externships, this time in New York, I could write to no more than eight sites. I still had the opportunity to turn back and pursue non-neuro placements, yet I decided to try out for five in hospitals whose neurology ranking varied from number 1 to 16 in New York. I also decided to throw in three general psych hospitals that weren't even in the ranking as safety choices.

When I drafted my cover letters, I decided to be honest about my fascination with the gut-brain axis and about how I wanted to become proficient in neuropsychology in order to eventually combine it with gastroenterology. People in the field know that this is a very weird and very random combination that may have easily led me to nowhere. I was pretty sure that I would only hear back from the general psych sites and that that would signify the end of my year-long neuro quest. A few days later, I had gotten interview offers by all five neuro hospitals and zero by the general ones. So much for safety choices, I thought and went about preparing for the meetings.

If I can give any advice to anyone who wants it (aka no one), that is: CYBERSTALK the people who will interview you, their research, their current projects, their grants, their social media platforms (don't slip and like anything-then you're in real trouble), their site, their equipment, their labs, the insects on their walls, their third-grade teacher, where they went to summer camp, and when's their mom's name day. I once heard the CEO of a major Italian fashion brand (not Ferragamo), say that women need to be much more prepared than men in order to succeed and that this is why successful women are really successful and difficult to bring down.

During my time at the HuffPost, I wrote self-help articles, and although I eventually became a real-deal therapist, I still consider these my golden life-coaching days (as you are reading this, a psych professor is setting themselves on fire). Another thing that I want to say to female readers is that we are often socialised to shy away from complex things such as STEM, such as accounting, such as problems that need a thought-through practical solution, and we learn to say, "Oh, I don't know about that – I don't want to mess it up." You won't mess it up. Roll up your sleeves and learn. If we are to claim our seat at the table, we need to dispel ourselves from the misconception that people who are louder or who appear to be more confident (usually men) are actually more capable than us because we probably are just as capable, yet we don't give ourselves the opportunity to try.

Now that I've started talking about men and women sharing career fields, I need to mention what Jamal taught me.

69

Jamal was a social worker at the South African psychiatric hospital where I interned some years back. Jamal and the other therapists (including little intern me) would gather around a very serious Dr Tala, the group supervisor, who was an off-campus addition that would come and go every Thursday morning to check in with how we were handling our cases.

Jamal disliked Dr Tala's tone and sex-focused psychoanalytic interpretations of every breath we drew in our therapy rooms and decided to rebel against her without her ever realising it. A cold August Thursday (we were south of the equator), right after the supervisor had exited the room, Jamal instructed us to sit back down and laid out the game plan. He was going to include one new client in next week's supervision. "Which one?" asked Raisa, an unsuspecting therapist who had just transferred her therapeutic license and had moved from Dubai to Cape Town with her husband and two young children.

"You want to know which one?" asked Jamal. "One that we will make up," he said. I looked at him, mouth aghast as I still to this day feel like psychoanalytic therapists can smell insincerity from miles apart. Headstrong as he was, he marched in the room next Thursday with a missing-tooth smile and danced into his seat right across Dr Tala.

"Any new…" the supervisor began, but Jamal interrupted her mid-word and said,

"YES! We have this new client – really exciting case, a boy aged 20, that came in two days ago." We were all ready to have our therapeutic rights evoked, but we were also curious to see what would happen next. Some were turning

70

red from embarrassment, and others couldn't hold back from grinning ear to ear.

"Andy!" Jamal continued. "Andy did the intake – it really took him two full hours, and there were noises coming from the room. The boy even broke a painting we had on the wall. You know which one?" He turned to me. "The one with the waves and the fish. Oh my God, Andy, I can't wait for you to tell us what happened in that room!"

Radio silence. Poor Andy didn't know what to do, everyone was scanning each other's faces, and I had surrendered to the idea that I would be sent back to Greece earlier than expected. After a full three minutes, Dr Tala turned to Andy and said, "Was the patient too much for you to handle? I know you often have trouble conceptualising difficult cases from the get-go."

Andy may have been quiet, but he wasn't going to stand back and have his skills attacked. He cleared his throat, straightened his back, and started speaking. "20-year-old, Afrikaan boy came in as an emergency on Tuesday night. Presenting problem: excessive giggliness. The boy laughs to the point of self-wetting, has no underlying neurological deficits, yet finds everything hilarious. The intake took so long because I couldn't get a word out of him. He was all – how old are you – how old am AAAHA HAHAHAHAHAHAH. HAHAHAHAHAHAH.HAHAHA. HAHAHAHAHAHAH.Hahahahahah. Then HAAAAAAAA hahahahah, and so on. The painting did, in fact, break, only because he is a pushy laugher. You know the type! The ones that jump around as if they'll have to go potty, then lean against whatever they find, arms flailing and all? That's him. And there went the fish!"

"Hmmm," said the supervisor while tears were running down most of our cheeks. "Sounds like an interesting case. It sounds like his ID (Freud alert) forces out of himself in the form of laughter because he's probably too afraid to express it in a sexual manner that could be linked to castration anxiety that may date back to his time as a boy and to his oedipal complex (incest alert) because he was in competition with his father for the mother's love."

"Absolutely not," said Jamal. "The boy was raised on a farm at the feet of Constantia Mountain, where a leopard owner found him under a baobab tree. No mother or father to fall in love with."

The case of the laughing boy developed into a graphic biography of love, lust, and so, so much pant-wetting throughout my stay at the internship. The team derived great joy from this evolving tail and partook in magical storytelling that began as a hoax but then turned into a collective narrative.

Although Jamal didn't teach me much about real-life cases, he taught me about the magic of imagination and how it can create realistic stories that fit quite well in stressful clinical interrogations (otherwise known as supervision). When I was preparing for my five important neuropsych interviews, I had suspected that I needed to get ready to present a case that would showcase not only my experience but also the relevance of that experience with what the particular site had to offer. No, dear reader, I did not present the case of the laughing boy but damn! He would have been such a great fit.

As I interviewed in hospitals that saw people with Parkinson's, Alzheimer's, Epilepsy, Cancer, Traumatic Brain Injuries, and other diagnoses, and even though I had worked with patients with most of them in the past, I decided that rehearsing them as they were would not cut it. I thus bought five mini whiteboards, drew a sketch of each patient with their respective diagnosis on them, did research on what these new hospitals would look at, what papers the supervisors had published on each pathology, and started adding information to every story (for interview purposes only – that's a serious offence if you do it in real life so stay away from trouble!). I was channelling my inner Jamal and was pursuing the magic of the laughing boy in all my patients.

Every night for over a month, I would hop in the shower, practice my case presentations and ask myself questions that might come up during interviews. "Are they a good candidate for Deep Brain Stimulation? How old is their partner? Do they have support at home? What's their favourite food, and why souvlakia? What's their least favourite show, and why Game of Thrones? Do they have a history of other conditions? What about infections?" I would sometimes wake up midway through the night to keep notes of ideas I had while sleeping. The interviews went well. The only downside was, no one ever asked me for a case presentation…

Chapter 13
Fun Gut Facts I Gathered
Through the Interview Process

Besides rehearsing laughing-boy-like cases for my neuropsych interviews, I decided to research the relationship between the gut and the conditions that each hospital would focus on. While this was a throw spaghetti on the wall and see if it sticks strategy, I did come up with quite some gems about the gut and neurodegeneration that I'll share with you here. My first interview was with the neurology department of a major NY hospital that mostly focused on motor disorders. Parkinson's is one example, and Epilepsy is another, although Epilepsy is a very heterogeneous disorder that may not commence from motor centres always. Some researchers have found that Epilepsy that derives from the limbic system can cause feelings of hyper-religiosity, thoughts of having met God, and even a sense of being on an actual rollercoaster of emotions within two minutes or less[26]. I don't know why I elaborated on this here (I'm quite the chatter), so let me catch my train of thought. This department advertised itself as a centre that provided ample opportunities, one of which, I read, was 'ion testing'. Now, I had zero ideas what that meant, but

I had a feeling that this would give me the leeway I needed to claim my spot at the program. After extensive research, I found that another department of the same hospital had purchased 'ion genomic testers', which were basically an elaborate 23andme machine if I got it correctly.

This information really excited me as I had already dwelled on nature versus nurture hypotheses about the gut-brain axis. Twin studies that explore the gut found that even monozygotic twins, the samest among the same, had vastly different microbiomes in between them[21]. Researchers claimed that this can explain why one twin can get cancer while the other doesn't and why one may get Alzheimer's while the other doesn't. This insight is particularly interesting in considering the nature/nurture conundrum at underprivileged parts of the world, including the aforementioned food deserts where all dietary choices are hyper-processed and thus unhealthy. If a mother gets a disease rooted in inflammation, such as diabetes, for example, or even a neurodegenerative one (given that these have also been described as inflammatory diseases by some researchers during the past decade) and consumes a certain type of diet, or endures intense stress (both factors that can cause gut dysbiosis), then their son or daughter may be consuming the exact same diet, and they may be enduring the same levels of stress, thus creating a pathology cycle and eventually getting a similar diagnosis.

Genetic predisposition is so complex yet so interesting in gut-brain health, and it can even signify that someone who is predisposed to celiac disease, for example (my peoples' tastebud condemnation), may have been undiagnosed for years, thus leading to inflammation and to neuroinflammation, thus making them more susceptible to developing neurodegenerative disorders[27]. All of this information made me super excited for the job interview and for getting to meet these people who would allow me to do ion testing, according to the website. The interview was, in fact, very interesting, yet it turns out that ion testing was a misspell, and they didn't know what it was. They did, however, take genetics into consideration when building integrative neurological assessments, and that's all that mattered.

My second interview was with another super exciting hospital that had an Epilepsy and Stroke focus. Stroke, as I figured out pre-interview, relates to the gut in a magnificent way. Apparently, when people have a stroke, there is a sequence of bodily processes that occur, as the body is fighting to restore homeostasis. One of these processes that follow a stroke is gut dysbiosis. Researchers have noticed that gut dysbiosis may lead to a leaky gut syndrome, which means that the toxins that are in the gut (because yes, this body part does carry the dirtiest load of the human body while also creating magic) permeate the intestinal walls and get into the bloodstream. This sequence of events then causes neuroinflammation that may result in further neurological damage in peoples' brains[28]. What this means is that when people have a stroke, yes, they may have some initial, large, or small neurological damage, yet the gut then causes even more secondary trauma that scientists are now trying to prevent through the timely use of probiotics, among other techniques.

What is true about stroke may also apply to Traumatic Brain Injuries (TBIs) and secondary, gut-related neurological damage. In the case of TBIs, an additional factor makes the toxins permeate the intestinal walls at a much faster pace. That is that when someone hits their head, they get a full-body experience of the trauma. It is very difficult for a person to acquire an injury that is isolated to their brain unless someone has made them lie down on a lab and has taken a swing on them, in which case, they must have made it to the storyline of a Law and Order episode and never lived to watch it air. When the entire body is shaken up by a TBI, intestinal walls become much more permeable to toxins[29], and a similar cycle to the one precipitated after a stroke takes place.

Moving on to my third interview, this was at a fully Epilepsy focused centre (I promise there is a versatility of cases when you get in, but the major categories are the same and thank God – for treatments' sake). What I learned about Epilepsy and the gut is that researchers have found that people who have refractory Epilepsy, that is, drug-resistant Epilepsy, and who usually result to surgeries including lobectomies and other, less invasive procedures, also have a composition of gut microbiota (the bacteria in there), where the bad prevail the good[30]. They have thus concluded that one's gut composition may affect their susceptibility to having epileptic seizures and, treatment-wise, they have found that people with refractory (again, drug-resistant) Epilepsy may benefit from gut-focused approaches that may help them alleviate some of the symptoms of the disorder[31].

My fourth interview was at the neurological department of a large cancer centre. When it comes to cancer, there is the commonplace belief (and scientific finding) that prolonged gut dysbiosis can lead to different types of cancer, the most common ones being oesophageal and colon cancer[32]. One positive research-based fact is that people living in South Africa who consume a fibre-heavy diet have minimal levels of colin cancer[33]. Conclusion:

Eat your oats, people (remember the 30grams a day rule[12]).

Another important cancer-gut-related finding is that chemo mostly affects the brain, possibly creating cognitive challenges (and possibly not, so don't get alarmed – plus, there are remediation techniques including cognitive exercises and pharmacological treatment), but it also affects the gut[34]. In the gut, chemo tends to cause mucositis. Mucositis is a painful inflammation of the mucous membranes that are lining the digestive tract, and research suggests that, as in the case of Stroke and TBIs, this gastrointestinal dysfunction may lead to further neurological damage. My fifth interview was at a neurological department focused on all of the above, so I rinsed and repeated.

Chapter 14
(Laughing) Boy Interrupted

Four months after flying home from Cape Town, I got a phone call from Jamal saying that he wanted me to testify to Dr Tala (dramatic choice of wording, I know), that he had made up the tail of the laughing boy and that we had all played along. "She wint heuurt ye in eeeny weeey Deeephne!" he said in my politically incorrect impression of his South African accent (I've been told worse. A friend of my dad's said, I sound like Arianna Huffington).

"What happened?" I inquired, and Jamal went on to explain how the team had kept up the laughing boy tail, with updates every single Thursday morning. They had said he turned from an inpatient to an outpatient, then an inpatient, then an outpatient again. Andy was the one who got them all in trouble when he said that the boy wanted to be committed again because his abs were becoming too toned and his bladder too weak from laughing. The team said that they had transferred him to his new room after moving him out of his first – assigned one. Steven, they said, his newly assigned roommate who had Tourette's, would scream "DIEEEE" at the sound of a giggle and would upset the nurses.

"Jeez Eande!" said Jamal, as he went on to explain that Dr Tala grew worried that they had recklessly ignored the 2x hospitalisation limit and had let the poor boy come in again. If you're noticing that Jamal's accent changed through these chapters, it's because he would suffer from 'stress-indeeeeced eaccent eagraveahshion!' as he explained every time he got upset.

"You have messed up! You have all messed up!" Dr Tala said and then announced that she, as the supervisors' supervisor and the grandest authority in place, would be the one who would speak to the boy to explain that he would have to be released according to hospital and insurance policies. "Let him spend the night and bring him here tomorrow morning so we can talk."

Resourceful as he was, Jamal spent the remainder of his Thursday trying to recruit one of his cousins to play out the laughing boy. "Leaaaughh! Leaahghhh you stiiiuuuupid frog!" he would scream at his cousin Tommy who skipped a day of Engineering school to help his cousin and a bunch of out-of-line therapists.

And oh, did Tommy laugh, and he laughed loudly and incessantly, all through Thursday's practice and through his sit down with Dr Tala who he could not hear over his grandiose-turned breathless – turned grandiose again – turned Tommy blue – laughs. Exhausted and impatient, Dr Tala left the giggle-echoing room, met with the therapists who had paused all of their schedules to start packing their belongings, sweat on her forehead and all, and said, "We need to take the boy to Metropolitan. He needs to be assessed by specialised neurologists. I think he'll need electrical stimulation. He is utterly dysfunctional! Cannot hold a proper conversation. I'm calling the ambulance."

You can imagine what happened next. No, Jamal did not confess to what he had done and nor did any of the rest of them. Kind of you to think so, though. Tommy was taken to the neurological headquarters (laughter died down when he saw the paramedics), where they found nothing and decided to move him on to the psych ward. That's when Tommy's mom called Jamal, threatened to set a gypsy curse on him and had him repent and self-flagellate until the boy got back to his box-drawing mornings at the University of Cape Town, over Madiba Circle.

Chapter 15
Business Plan According to My Grandma (Yes, This Is Actually Her Book, Vicariously Written Through Me)

Now that I've gone over my strategies for staying at a high level of training as a woman in a scientific field, I am ready to let you in on the advice that my grandma, a double doctor, has given me, in order to strategise my way into success:

- Never write a book titled 'Brain's got the shits again' because it will be social suicide in scientific circles
- Never mention you were modelling to pay for school and if someone does find out, make sure you clarify there was ZERO nudity involved
- Marry a gastroenterologist as you'll be able to do gut-brain research together
- Come to think of it again, you never know where their hands have been so better marry a psychiatrist
- Publish more academic articles

- Get a teaching position along with working at the neurological department of a prestigious hospital (in the developed world Teri, or this time you WILL get tuberculosis)
- Interact with medical teams, see what they do and appreciate it
- Quit your job as a neuropsychologist
- Go to med school because everything else is witchcraft

Chapter 16
Which Medical Fields are Most Marry-Worthy and Why, According to My Grandma

If you enjoyed the don't marry a gastroenterologist tip, here is my grandma's accumulated knowledge about the subfields of medicine that produce the best brides and grooms. She married a dentist and she never stopped smiling (jk, her expressions were mostly lukewarm until grandpa passed):

- Dermatologist: marry them if you really love them and want to spend a lot of time with them
- Surgeon: marry them if you love them but are easily annoyed by them to have a lot of free time to yourself
- Anesthesiologist: marry them after doing a thorough background check because you never know who they've roofied
- Pathologist: marry them and you'll be caressed by the hands that have touched a dead body. And not a fresh out of surgery one. A real deal morgue corpse
- Urologist: same as gastroenterologist

- Gynaecologist: marry them but get another one for freedom's sake ;)
- Neurologist: marry them if you're a neuropsychologist and haven't yet realised who the real neuro bosses are. Then quit and apply to med school.

Sphincter Fairy

Chapter 17
Excuses to Not Show Up for
a Date/Appointment

As a person who spent a good 55% of a decade lying in bed due to tiredness that is now miraculously gone, I have acquired a list of skills that some of you dear readers may find useful. First of all, if you too are feeling down, I truly hope you feel better soon and I hope this book helps you smile at least a little (do it now you son-of-a-bitch!). Second, if you're lacking energy and wish to cancel on friends / a prospective date, or even an official commitment, I am not here to make you feel worse about it because I've been there multiple times, and I am happy to share some insight. Not about getting up and pursuing social interaction. No. We can talk about that at different times. Now I'll only share my catch phrases that have gotten me out of commitments I made when I was younger and overestimated my energy levels. So here they go:

- My tires are flat and I am waiting for car roadside assistance
- My car is leaking and I am waiting for car roadside assistance

- I am in the vehicle of car roadside assistance, that is driving my car to a faraway lot where they will fix all that is wrong with it
- My mom accidentally locked me in the house
- My brother accidentally locked me in the house
- My cat's in the hospital (I have no cats)
- The neighbour was robbed and asked for help (I live on a desolate farm)
- My grandpa showed up unexpectedly (both my grandfathers are dead but I'm sure they're happy to help)
- I forgot I had a zoom meeting with my friend from Australia. Melbourne in particular!
- I have a fever (don't use it and jinx yourself in covid times)
- I have a cough (don't covid jinx yourself – keep it for later)
- I forgot I had a term paper to turn in
- My brother is getting a divorce (it was finalised two years ago)
- I got the shits again (yay for our title – okay, embarrassing but effective!)
- I have a family emergency that I'll tell you about when we meet next (which may be never but if you do, you'll find something when the time comes)
- There's water all over the kitchen floor
- The dog is on the kitchen floor and doesn't know how to swim
- Now there's fish all over the floor, and we're a vegan household You're welcome! Enjoy your Netflix!

Chapter 18
Out of Couch Coaching

While self-help journals columns may seem close to actual psychology, there is a huge disregard of any type of coaches by licensed therapists. The reason is simple. To become a life coach you can set up a blog on WordPress and start, whereas to become a psychologist, at least in the US, you need to get a BA, an MSc, then a PhD, do an internship, sit for licensing exams, then do a year of postdoc and then apply for licensure. That's a LOT of time and a LOT of money, plus a LOT of opportunities to drop out if you wish.

As a blogger for the HuffPost, I definitely verged on the coaching side, although I had a BA (it was on Cultural Studies, yes I did think that money grew on trees at the time. It's paper!). During my interviews for the MSc and the PhD, I kept saying that I wanted to substantiate what I wrote because it's a large responsibility to tell people what to do. I got in both programs and then figured out that therapists are NOT to tell people what to do under most circumstances (unless they're about to become a danger to themselves or to someone else. Then you let them know and call the police).

While psychologists seem to be unbiased witnesses of peoples' unfolding experiences, I have formed an inside notion (yet, I was a self-help blogger so feel free to disregard it if you wish), that therapists do, often have an opinion about what people should be doing. I have also noticed that this opinion slips out of them in sessions when they are the most tired or upset at their better halves or their children.

In any case, to become a neuropsychologist you first need to become a psychologist and I don't want my rights revoked so I'll stop with the risky insights. I will mention however that in a class where we were discussing therapists and life coaches, and although most of us, tired students, were ready to jump ship and sign up for WordPress, we realised that there is a 12-year training difference between us. Later in that day, we would go over cases to practice our therapy skills (this was an introductory course). The professor would read out clients' requests and they would want us to answer in a way that was consistent with that day's materials. These requests would vary from "tell me what to do with my screaming mom", "tell me if I should stay with my boyfriend", "tell me how old you are – you look too young to be doing this job", or "tell me what your cell is so we can hook up later" (that last one is a fast-track lose-your-license deal – just letting you know).

After we had spent a good forty minutes practising, the professor read out the following: "I am 17 years old and about to apply to schools. I want to become a psychologist, but I am too bored of books and don't think I'll be able to study a lot. I mostly enjoy playing computer games (okay – perhaps the terminology was different but I am not of this generation), and don't want to overdo it with school work. What should I do?"

As I mentioned earlier, most of us were tired from studying at the time so there were a couple of people who said "RUUUN", to address the request. Others said that studying for psychology wasn't as hard – they were casted away, out of class and deep into the mountains behind campus. I said they should try life coaching.

Now, this is one of the jokes that I laughed about on my own, as it didn't land in the context of the classroom. My laugh consists of a HAAAAAA!, followed by an inhale that sounds like half a hiccup (on repeat). I have always been the person who stops laughing and then randomly remembers the joke four hours later, amidst a scientific conference or a moment when someone has just shared something heartbreaking like – their cat's in the cat hospital. Trust me when I say, if no one joins my HAAAAAA! and half a hiccup during the time of the joke, no one and I mean NO ONE empathises with my repeated quarters of hiccups that precede it.

I would now like to dedicate this paragraph that is already unrelated to the topic of this book, to describe my favourite types of laughs. Better yet, I will quote Wikipedia that says, "Laughter can be classified according to: intensity – the chuckle, the titter, the giggle, the chortle, the cackle, the belly laugh, the sputtering burst; the overtness – snicker, snigger, guffaw; the respiratory pattern involved – snort" and so forth. Being Greek, I don't know what half of these words mean and I lack the energy to google them so please, dear reader, take a minute to consider what your best laugh sounds like and hey, give it a try. See what I did there? I made you think of a funny memory. You're welcome you silly goose.

While therapy isn't a place for advice, life-coaching definitely is and because I'm tired of pretending to not have an opinion for over five years now, I will momentarily and shamelessly put on my coaching hat to share what tricks have helped me get out of bed or stand the autoimmune-reduced tiredness, in case they can be helpful to someone currently dealing with depression or extreme giggliness syndrome, especially after this, hilarious, last paragraph. Isn't hilarious such a funny word? It makes me giggle just as the word 'yawn' makes me yawn. Did you just yawn too?

So here is my list of tricks to face some of what's weighing you down (hopefully not one of these Kardashian-endorsed weighted blankets. Or is this joke to 2015?):

- **Turn your shame into a short story.** Shame is an ever-present emotion (Thank you Brene Brown!), that's difficult to hack out of our systems. And maybe we shouldn't because true psychopaths are that shameless and we want all of us to make it out alive. Shame is also a feeling that flourishes on the battleground, as is a person with depression, intense anxiety, or any other mood disorder.

A few years ago and after I published my first book, I got a lot of followers on Facebook (I'm currently on a spiritual break from social media except Instagram – I need to know what Alec Baldwin's wife's yoga pose of the day is). This was around Christmas time so I started getting many, many messages from people sending holiday wishes. As I couldn't reply to everyone in one – or even five – sittings, I decided to post a story in which I thanked them and reciprocated the wishes. When I sat down for Christmas dinner, my dad said that I shouldn't have done that, without explaining why. By the way, people with Greek parents know that when they say you shouldn't have done something without explaining why

THEY ARE ROASTING YOU LIKE A LAMB ON EASTER LUNCH.

In any case, I got upset, truly, truly shameful, although I hadn't exactly realised where I was wrong, and also pretty bummed about having to spend Christmas Eve in a bad mood. Prolific as I was, I rushed to my childhood room, took out my laptop and started writing a short story about a high school vice-principal named Phaedra, who had just been caught locking a student she disliked in the bathroom so that she would recite a poem on stage in her place, and who was driving home in tears and anguish. I started taking note of her exact bodily sensations, how she wanted to crawl out of her skin, dig the earth and hide in it (translated Greek expression right here – you're welcome), and followed her until she got home, got even more upset my her father's comment who said she looked old, went to the kitchen and broke all plates.

Because my own shame hadn't been released by the last plate, we then went on to breaking fictional glasses, then coffee cups, bowls, eco-friendly, glass – Tupperware and finally, a salad spinner. Trust me, placing your shame in an evolving story gives you the opportunity to release it in any way you find the most satisfying, through words. Try it.

- **Nobody is thinking about you.** Another common misconception that I had when I was going through my health challenges, was that because I quit a loooot of jobs, moved back and forth from the US to Europe more than twice, couldn't maintain long term relationships because I truly didn't have the energy to do so, plus I was insecure about my ever-changing body, that made me feel less desirable at the time (now I like myself so much, I'm dangerous – jk but wouldn't that be amazing?), and I was having a hard time conveying to my friends exactly what was happening and why I was bailing on our plans, I felt like a weirdo. Not because I felt like a weirdo but because I was pretty sure that people would look at me and think, "She's just a mess. She has no clue where she's going in life and she's so boring."

At some point, however, and after surviving the semi-humiliation of flying to Boston to start my MBA, not even making it until the end of orientation week and then flying back to Greece for all the people who had said their goodbyes to me to walk by me bewildered and conscious not to ask anything triggering, I realised I was wrong. Not because if someone were to think of me, they wouldn't think I'm a weirdo, but because I was overestimating the amount of time that people spend thinking about others.

Think of your own experience. Yes, you may worry or think of your family's and friends' lives, okay, Kylie Jenner's too, but how much time do you actually spend in contemplation of other peoples' life choices? I mean, you have your own life to worry about, work too, probably school, your boyfriend or girlfriend, and all the shows that bring you joy. Realising that people don't actually think about others for long and if they do, they're actually missing out on their own lives, has truly liberated me from my self-consciousness about past and present failures. Fail like no one is watching, is my advice because no one is – at least that closely.

- **Memory is suggestible and re-encodable.** We had a very interesting 'Cognition and Affect course' on my first semester as a PhD student, that was presented by a professor who was against psychotherapy. They were a cognitive psychologist, yet they disliked the idea of therapy and while I initially thought that they were missing on the magic of our field, I eventually realised that they were on to something.

The suggestibility of memory is a notion that suggests (see what I did there?) that memories are continuously constructed. We all have that one friend who is an exaggerator, sees a cat pass the street, arrives at work and says it was a lion, then says the lion came to their window, then that the window was wide open and so the lion barfed in their direction and it was smelly. The more the exaggerators add, the more they encode the new versions of the story as memories until they eventually believe that the lion really did barf. In the context of therapy, or thinking about someone with a mood disorder, this whole idea may be saying that if you're feeling sad and rethink an otherwise happy or neutral memory, you may be turning it into a negative one. After being relieved from emotional distress that derived from my autoimmune condition (in my opinion), I started realising how many memories I had turned into negatives during that time, and how I could recode them as positive ones when thinking of them now that I'm happier. What I mean to say is, things are definitely not as shitty as they seem when you are depressed. Just keep that in mind.

- **We're all going to die someday.** Whenever I've found myself in stressful situations – e.g. during PhD admissions' interviews, or job interviews at the hospitals I mentioned, I use my tried and true strategy to distress. That is, I look around the room, scan it for people there, and then think "Huh. They'll die one day. Like they will actually be buried in the ground (that's an overgeneralisation from being a Greek Orthodox, ground burial is our second distinctive feature after a wild, wild premarital sex). Bugs will eat them."

Trust me when I say, this strategy works FAST. Not only do you start feeling bad for the poor interviewer, but then you also think that you'll one day die as well and you realise just how similar the two of you are. Put me in a room with Queen Elizabeth and I won't choke. Put me in a room with a Buddhist who believes in reincarnation and I will because they'll still be here after I'm lunch for the caterpillars. Can you imagine? I'm allergic to caterpillars! Depressed or happy, everyone's eventually turning into dust so, once again, ignore social judgment and dare for what you care.

- **Drop your negative friends.** Not literally. Just send them away. There are two types of friends I've decided to live without since finding my joy, and here's what these are. The first is the type of friends who are always so buuuuusyyyy, always so tiiiiireeeeed, always so neeeervouuuuus, always getting life's short end of the stick. I first heard that idea in a podcast, how being too busy, tired and burnt out is sort of a social accolade in our fucked up society (oops, lots of fucks going on in this paragraph) and that we can actually break that narrative and when someone asks how we are, say: very well – even if we're not.

In psychology, we usually encourage people to be genuine with their feelings but I tend to disagree, just in this case. If anyone and I mean, ANYONE spends more than two minutes thinking about how they feel, how they really, really feel, it may be easy for them to find a negative. Now, socially, it is more appropriate to disclose the negative feelings than the positive ones, or to match someone when they say they are feeling tired, being like "Omg mee tooooooo!" because once you share the good, people may think you're failing, are lobotomised and haven't figured out what's happening in the world, or are spoiled in some way. A friend of mine from the PhD who I shared this idea with, decided to respond to everyone in a positive way. She then got an email from her advisor saying, "How is your summer going?", to which she responded, "It's going wonderfully! I'm taking time for myself and I'm very happy to relax," to which the advisor responded, "I'm afraid you're falling back in research."

The second type of friends who are not bringing you any joy are your brutally honest friends. The ones who advertise themselves in that way and who make you really, really value their opinion and really, really care to impress them. Here's a fun little insight: they aren't the truth keepers of the world, they aren't experts in many things and even if they are, do not seek for their opinion unless their speciality is math or something. FUCK THEM. When someone says they are brutally honest what they are actually telling you, very, very, very clearly is that they are brutal and that they cannot wait for an opportunity to brutalise you or anyone else in the world. I've had many friends like that, and even mentors who I later left behind, who kept saying, ohhhh if I'm being brutally honest, I think you'll fail. I am very proud to say that while I have failed in many things, I have never failed in something that these people predicted I would. You don't need that kind of energy in your life, especially when you're trying to reestablish joy in it.

Chapter 19
Gut-Related Colloquial
Greek Expressions

Now that we've gone over feel-good strategies when being down, I want to make you smile. So here you go. You know how when you get a new dog, you think that no one has a similar one, and then you look around and suddenly realise that, oh my God, EVERYONE has the exact same dog? It's because your brain is now primed to recognise what's familiar. This can also explain the experience I had when I walked around Greece after my interest in all-things-gut was sparked. As Greeks, we have our own set of expressions that mean absolutely nothing to foreigners who listen to them and who try to translate them. About 60% of these expressions, I noticed, were gut-health related. More specifically:

- Gut-related gas expressions:
o I farted door-knobs (Έκλασα πόμολα): means, I was very afraid o He is a fart bathtub (Είναι κλασομπανιέρας): used to describe someone who is afraid a lot o From where does the mullet fart? (Από πού κλάνει το μπαρμπούνι;): used to express that

something is obviously incomprehensible o The bride farted and the wedding was over (Έκλασε η νύφη, σχόλασε ο γάμος): you can take this one literally

- Gut-related poop expressions:
o Shit high and watch (Χέσε ψηλά και αγνάντευε): means, be unperturbed, relax o He turned me the intestines (Μου γύρισε τα άντερα): means, he disgusted me o Anybody walking in the night steps on mud and shit (Όποιος τη νύχτα περπατεί, λάσπες και σκατά πατεί): means, you're looking for trouble
o When the shit blows on the wall (Όταν σκάσει το σκατό στον τοίχο) means when it's the point of no return
o Eat shit (Σκατά να φας): means exactly what it meant when Octavia Spencer said it on the Help o I did them on me (Τα έκανα πάνω μου): means I soiled myself, I was very afraid of It harvested me (Με θέρισε): it gave me diarrhoea o The old man goes from fall or from shit (Ο γέρος πάει ή από πέσιμο ή από χέσιμο): Old people often die due to fall-induced fractures, or to gastrointestinal problems
- Gut-related body part expressions:
o Like the monkey's ass (Σαν τον κώλο της μαϊμούς): means, very ugly o Like the barber's ass (Σαν τον κώλο του κουρέα): means, quite nice
- Gut-related food consumption expressions:
o The fat priest ate fat lentils, why fat priest did you eat fat lentils? (Ο παππάς ο παχύς έφαγε παχιά φακή, γιατί παππά παχύ, έφαγες παχιά φακή;): used as a tongue twister o They don't chew (Δεν μασάνε): means, they are not afraid o Does the goat chew salted

fish roe? (Μασάει η κατσίκα ταραμά;): used to exhibit a lack of fear, courage to Slow the cabbages! (Σιγά τα λάχανα!): means, so what?

o About appetite, pumpkin pie (Περί ορέξεως κολοκυθόπιτα): means, everyone can do as they please.

Chapter 20
Gut-Related Colloquial English Expressions

Hey, there English-speaking friends. Have you been laughing with Greek gut phrases? I'm about to let you in on a Greek secret. You know Mr Portokalos from My Big Fat Greek Wedding and how he'd say kimono is a Greek word because it comes from the Greek word "hemonas – which is mean winter, and what do you wear in winter to not get cold? Kimono. Kimono – hemonas – there you go"? All Greeks laugh about that. But we laugh about that when another Greek is mentioning it. If you're not Greek and make a joke about Mr Portokalos, or Toula, or Voula, we will get offended. It's like when you're roasting your brother to a friend, and then they go, "Yeah, he sucks," and then you go, "HEY! I can say it!" Because Greeks are masters at getting offended and at getting back at people who have offended us, here's a list of your own English gut expressions:

- Know your shit
- Eat that shit
- Drink that shit

- Learn that shit
- Good shit
- Bad shit
- No shit
- Deep shit
- Tough shit
- Full of shit
- Shit stirrer
- Scare the shit out of
- Don't give a shit
- Shitstorm
- Look like shit
- Feel like shit
- Lose my shit – The shit!
- Shitty
- Shithead – Oh shit!
- Bullshit
- Shit hits the fan
- Shit-faced, and, lastly, a life-coaching one:
- Get your shit together.

Dr Rear-Gear

Chapter 21
A Little Bit Better

Now that I've shamelessly gone over my tiredness-and-sadness-fighting moves, my gut-inspired business plans, and my grandma's tips on smart marriages, I wanted to share what my back-to-health-and-joy journey actually looked like. Remember when I said that two days after I stopped eating dairy and gluten, I felt a change? That is absolutely true, yet my body still needed time to recover, find a normal – unbloated state to live in, and I needed time to unlearn my tired inclinations and excuses to avoid life.

Have you heard Kanye West or Kim Kardashian describe how contentment is better than happiness because you can't always be happy, but you can be content? Well, first of all, content as a feeling, content as a book's index, and contempt, are three words that I love to use interchangeably because my English isn't just that impeccable. But I googled it, and I know that content as a feeling is what I want to discuss here. Anyway, I used to hear these celebrities advertise their strive for contentment, and I truly wanted to partake in that. I tried to find silver linings, write down three things that I'm grateful for each day (didn't really do the trick), think of others that had it way worse than me, yet nothing truly led me to that optimal, fine-balanced emotional state.

When I changed my diet, I still didn't experience contentment. I swear. I jumped right to joy, like a tall enough six-year-old riding their first rollercoaster in Disneyland. I jumped to joy like a height person jumps in an Amsterdam canal or like the laughing boy faced Dr Tala before being transferred to the psych ward.

I used to be the person who was always annoying from finding the negative, and then I went straight to the person who's always annoying for finding the positive. Others still dislike me, but I do live in a state of glee for a while now, and I really hope this won't go away. In any case, reestablishment of joy wasn't an issue for me – although it was for my surrounding people whose eyes have since rolled out of their faces – yet my body took a good five months to feel unperturbably normal again. As I mentioned under "Art of the Bloat", weighting in and seeing that I had gained even a minimal amount of weight will discourage me for the rest of the day and would keep me from trying to go for a walk or being sociable.

Even if I hadn't gained any weight, feeling super bloated and experiencing intense joint pain was also keeping me back.

I used to be an all-or-nothing person, and that's what held me back from a full life when having active celiac disease. I would quit going out or even trying at the slightest feeling of tiredness, pain, or bloating, and I would stay in bed until the feeling was gone, which could be weeks or months later. When I first started noticing changes in all my physical symptoms, after implementing lifestyle and dietary changes, I got too excited fast. I thought that my body would return to normal in a week, that I would never feel bloated again, and that nothing could disturb my gut health in the years to come. As you can imagine, I was wrong, and not only did my body take its sweet time to recover, yet symptoms flared back and aggressively so, after taking antibiotics (without probiotics at the time) for my ear infection. Something that truly helped me break the cycle of over-excitement about recovery and then heartbrokenly giving up again was the notion of 'a little bit better'. Whenever I began to feel discouraged, I would pause, and I would ask myself. "Are you as bloated as you were this time last year, or is it a little bit better? Are you as tired as you were, or are you a little bit better? Are you as discouraged as you were, or are you a little bit better?" Every time, a little bit better absolutely resonated with my experience, and that kept me going and going, breaking out of my comfort zone every single day. When it comes to physical and mental health, thinking in 'a little bit betters' is something I wholeheartedly endorse.

Chapter 22
Monophobia and the Day
I Stopped Being Vegan

It is currently Spring, as I am writing these pages, and our garden is filled with caterpillars. I may get anaphylactic at the sight of them, but our four-month-old dog, who just moved in, seems to think they are home-produced green liquorice that she loves to chew on. Ira, our dog, pics up the caterpillars one by one, tastes them, and then spreads her jaws open and lets them roll over her tongue and onto the ground. That's exactly how my friends and family tasted my first gluten-dairy-soy-free recipes. Tongue extended rollout onto the plate. My cousin even threw a handful of lentil Bolognese out the window and onto our neighbour's bald spots as he was watering the lawn. The neighbour thought a cat had gone number two on him from a tree. You get the idea...

When my grandfather passed away, my grandma (I know, I know, but I haven't mentioned her in over five chapters, okay?) got back together with her first love, a super tall dentist with a passion for healthy, tasteless food. They had a summer home together where they would meet during the weekends and where they would read the newest trends about what to eat to live to 150. Let's just say I have inherited my grandma's inexistent cooking skills that were also matched by her boyfriend's ineptitude in the kitchen. That didn't hold them back, however, as they bought all the suggested longevity ingredients and ate them uncooked, one after the other. How they never gagged, I don't know, yet their breakfasts would look something like this: a carrot, a teaspoon of honey, a pinch of cinnamon, a pinch of cayenne pepper, ground cumin, a handful of spinach, half a peach, a fourth of a banana, red peppers, a fourth of a fork, a piece of the Tupperware, some soap from the washing machine and water from the car's windshield wipers.

That's similar to what my food list consisted of during my first weeks of joy and misery until I started googling the health benefits of such a stale and nauseating diet. If I'm going to suffer, I thought, I'd rather feel good about it. And so I googled and googled until I watched a YouTube video about Instagram accounts that share amazing gluten, vegan recipes (because I already knew how to roast a chicken). My favourites still are @deliciouslyella and @thehappypear, and they truly shed light on the endless possibilities of beauty within the staleness of natural food.

Week after week, I was excited to try out different, abundant, colourful recipes that these pages suggested, from homemade quinoa pizza to beetroot pancakes. A change I was noticing was that I was slowly becoming used to and was actually craving this type of food. I haven't eaten chocolate since a looooong time ago, as there aren't any options available where I live, and I thought this would make me miserable, yet I'm just fine. The reason behind this is that, without realising it, I was retraining my tastebuds to

113

acknowledge and appreciate the taste of natural, mostly unprocessed foods.

I was super excited to try all of this out during the summer months, yet, come winter, I noticed that I wanted to retreat back to what I knew and to resort to just a couple, simple recipes that I would repeat day in and day out. Remember my math formula for one healthy recipe that I was hoping to create? Well, there's a good reason behind that. Ever since I was a child, I always truly, truly appreciated knowing what to expect from a particular food. Repeating plates and snacks truly comforted me, and I found the familiar tastes very soothing and rewarding. That's why I spent weeks eating the same ice cream cone as I mentioned earlier in this book.

My recipes were abundant, colourful, and beautiful when the available fruits and vegetables were easy to get (i.e. when my family members would enjoy going to the farmers market instead of me), yet they lacked versatility come December. I tried to create different dahls and summer rolls using vastly different ingredients, yet the strength of the taste had subsided for many of the ingredients, and they all ended up feeling like the exact same dish.

Unencouraged as I was, to keep on pursuing innovation, I chose three good recipes to repeat through winter: a morning oat bowl with frozen bananas, whichever other fruit is available, almond milk, and cinnamon, tomato-based dahl with lentil spaghetti, black beans, veggie broth, baby corn, and whichever vegetable is available, and a mushroom-based, peanut butter, tahini, noodle plate with whichever herb is available.

These options may sound tasty and healthy, yet they weren't the only thing I ate. I also LOVED pre-packaged

114

quinoa puffs that I had in tons until they too exacerbated my celiac as they contain some particles that, when eaten in large quantities, can be misread as gluten by my gut. After quinoa puffs were out, too, I bought Eat Real Veggie Strips that are a little too oily for my preferences, yet they are all that I have left. Plain peanut butter causes me acid reflux, but it's worth it, and then there is one last thing that I eat, and that drew me away from veganism after I realised I could have it.

After my ear infection and my antibiotics round, I was so tired, foggy and bloated, that I felt like my dietary interventions weren't sufficient to help me recover fast enough. This was one of the times when we really want something steady and filling to lift our spirits. As I was walking with my mom near our once-favourite bakery in Athens, she said, "I would buy you meringues, but you wouldn't eat them." I stopped her right then and there and learned that meringues' classic recipe entails sugar, another type of sugar, egg whites, and lots of whisking. "I don't even like chickens," I said, marched into that bakery, bought myself a three-layered box of mouth-watering meringues, and told the baker I was pregnant when they asked what I'd do with a human-sized meringue aggregation (I was not pregnant). It was ecstasy.

Chapter 23
Bloat Yoga

Dating a European person, as another European person living in New York is pretty common. We aren't exactly chauvinistic but there is some comfort in knowing that we all come from the same continent where corn syrup kale and childhood diabetes are not a thing. The majority of us carry ourselves with our own, distinctive accents unless you are my ex-boyfriend who vigorously practised in front of a mirror, to get rid of their Spanish tone. If you were to hear him speak, you would never assume he's not from Denver, as he not only divested himself from his European tone, yet he practised to perfection, through watching all nine seasons of the Dynasty.

What Thomas was missing, however, was an appreciation for the international version of English, that all non-native speakers have built-in other to communicate with one another. This language isn't always grammatically correct, but it is loud, it is slow, and it is clear. It doesn't matter if you're from Sri Lanka or Rome. If you know some English, you'll do well.

That's why they call it Engl-ish. It's an approximation of what the real thing sounds like. In any case, Thomas was into this whole healthy living vibe but he was suffering from intense heartburn and bloating after drinking green juices and running along the Hudson every morning. After reading that yoga could help debloat him, he signed us up for a sunrise session in a tiny, smelly Soho studio. When we got in, he tried to find the instructor and ask them to show us exercises that would help with bloating. To his surprise, the instructor had just moved to Manhattan from New Delhi, where he taught Hatha Yoga (I'm not a yogi so I don't know what this means). The instructors' accent sounded exactly like he had just moved to Manhattan from New Delhi, where he taught Hatha Yoga.

What's telling about Thomas's commitment to his long-sought Denver accent, however, is that even though he could speak Engl-ish, to match his international conversational partner, is that he was unyielding. He started off by saying "Thank you so much for meeting with me Mr Gnanasekaran. I'm afraid my stomach has been quite distended over the past few weeks. This could result from overconsumption of green goods; spinach, kale and the like. I was wondering if you would be so kind as to suggest some functional training that would help me relieve the pressure I am experiencing." The kind man looked at Thomas, then at me, then at Thomas again, smiling and said, "YyyyyoooOOOOghhhA!" Thomas tried again, in fact, he tried for a good fifteen minutes but his accent never once broke to explain things in a simpler manner, nor did he use his hands to gesture to what he meant.

My boyfriend was sweaty before the class had even started, and I was enjoying the sight of him, as the instructor patiently repeated "YyyyooogghhA, yyyy OOOooo GG hhhhhHA!" over and over again. "Ay, ay, ay." said Thomas and he remembered where he came from and what all the rest of us need to do to convey our messages in a multilingual world. "Estomago BAAAAD. Baaaad," he said while moving his hand around his gut. "Estomago PRRRrrrrt" he kept going.

The sight was hilarious, the instructor understood nothing and so we googled anti-bloating yoga poses when we got home. What came up was pretty simple and straightforward, so I'm adding a description here in case you too suffer from a distended estomago from time to time.

- **Do the twist and shout.** Or don't shout because they'll kick you out of the yoga retreat. Omg, already laughing at the image of that. Okay, so if you're lying down, head to the sky like you're counting stars on a roof with your first love at 13, extend your left hand as if you were closing your first love's mouth, telling them to shut up so that you could concentrate on counting. After that, bend your left leg and place it over your right leg that's still extended as if you're threatening your love that you'll go meet Mike at the ice cream shop if they don't stop. Keep your head to the left (looking at your love thinking if the roof's a good place for them to kiss you). Stay there for a while, then mentally place your love on your right side and repeat. Stay for as long as you want. I usually hold these positions until I feel like something's happening bloat-wise.

- **Hear the PRRrrrrrrrt.** Lie down, head to the sky, bend both knees and pull them to your chest. The name of the exercise is pretty self-explanatory so just stay there, or hug your knees, and rock them from side to side until you hear it. I know Thomas did.

- **Leapfrog without the leap.** When I was visiting my twin brother's home a while back, and we were ready to hit the road for a full-day hike, he said, "Hold on one minute, I really need to go." Then he dropped his jeans and kept his boxers in place, and started squatting like these were the TRX Olympics. When I asked him what he was doing, he said that this really helped him go and if I hadn't tried it, I was missing out. Little did I know at the time, but a similar pose was presented for anti-bloating on google (always a credible source). Google said, squat like a frog, so really near the ground, stay there, hug your open knees with your hands and wait, again until you hear the PRRrrrrt. At this point, I would just say, move and twist your body around until you hear the PRRRrrrrrt. It's the only trick.

Exercise is advertised as a pivotal pillar (see what I did there, Fancy Nancy?) of gut health. I am the poster child for abandoned fitness resolutions, so this was a challenging one for me to figure out. I appreciate the anti-bloating yoga but that's pretty much it. What I can do, however, is either walk a lot when I'm outdoors or walk a lot on a treadmill, pretending that I'm outdoors. Walking truly is the only form of exercise I appreciate and that is easy for me to commit to. That's why, when covid hit, I decided that that's all I expected of me. I would try to walk 10,000 steps a day which is about 7.5 to 8km and if I only got two or three a day, that would still be great. By simplifying my rules and expectations of myself, I definitely was able to incorporate some movement into my day (although 8km take me an hour and a half but I don't have kids and I've kept up with the Kardashians already so I have time).

Chapter 24
Dairy-Soy-Gluten-Free
Sex(Y) Lives

Have you heard of that saying that goes "You make love like you eat?" Public service announcement: You don't. Or at least I hope so because I'd be doomed. Technically, I wouldn't be the one being doomed but okay. Thus far, I have mentioned my German and my Spanish, vegan, yoga appreciating partners but I am sure that not everyone who follows a similar diet to mine finds someone like-minded to date. There aren't that many of us out there so fingers crossed that I'll get another one in the future.

However, Albert and Thomas definitely helped with my health journey, each in their own way, so I'd like to mention how, here. If you don't want to hear it, feel free to skip ahead but there's not much of the book left so PSYCH! By the way, I really don't know what PSYCH means exactly but I feel like I'm entitled to use it as a psychology PhD candidate, you know? Anyway. Here's a list of what these guys taught me, in mixed order:

- **Kiss contamination.** One of the most disconcerting facts that Albert figured out after googling celiac disease on his outdated Motorola under a camping tent, was that if you are a gluten-free celiac and your partner eats gluten, they can contaminate you through kissing. To which I said, "The hell with it – I've eaten gluten for 25 years already so I'll risk it." To which he said ABSOLUTELY no, which I wasn't sure was for me or for his inclination to radical health trends. In any case, we had dinner with my family one night and when he turned down a slice of bread that my dad had offered him, he turned to him and said "Meeeiiister Spayrooupooulos? Yiouuu heave miiiyyy werd, sir. I shall nieever contaminate yiiiouuurr daughtiiieeer with gluen! NIEMALS!"
- **Self-nudging nudgers.** Thomas was not only a self-propelled native speaker but he was also a connoisseur of all things wellness (all but how to say bloated in Engl-ish). When I asked him about how he was so disciplined in doing his five miles run every single day, he talked to me about 'Nudge', a book by Richard H. Thaler. Thaler, he explained was showcasing how healthy choices can be made over others when a person creates an environment that makes them easy to do. To simplify, Thomas said that even though he wasn't always in the mood for a run, he eventually realised that simple things would discourage him from doing it, such as having to pick and wear workout clothes or selecting songs in his playlist. He insisted that having his clothes ready from the night before, taking the time to make a

thought-through playlist that he actually enjoyed running to, and leaving his running shoes right near his door made him skip a lot of preparing and just get out the door.

- **A mental health pantry guide.** Albert's and my relationship lasted for a while and overlapped with my Nutritional Psychology training. During that training, I learned about which foods are good for which mental illness and although I wasn't very impressed nor convinced, Albert kept notes as he wished to publish a mental health pantry guide, depending on peoples' moods of the day. While I'm not sure he grasped the essence of the training, or how mental illness is different from a mood drop, I didn't want to dishearten him or make fun of his very own business idea (see how I didn't claim this one as one of my own?). What Albert wanted you to know, is that every mood has its remedy. More specifically:

  o **For depression:** eat oysters and mussels, seafoods, and organ meats (this was difficult for my vegan boyfriend to phathom but I'll leave it in).

Antidepressant plant foods are leafy greens, lettuce, peppers and cruciferous veggies such as broccoli, Brussels sprouts or cauliflower[35] o **For anxiety:** eat fermented foods[36] (try making them too, it's fun and soul-crushing if you're actively hungry), Brazil nuts, soybeans and mushrooms that contain selenium[37], fatty-fish that contain omega 3s[38], pumpkin seeds for potassium[39], dark chocolate for tryptophan that leads to serotonin production and magnesium[40], turmeric[41], and yoghurt that acts similarly to probiotics for gut-brain health[42].

Wrapping It Up

Chapter 25
What This Book Has Taught You About Gut Health

- Aim for 30 different plants per week
- Aim for 30 grams of fibre per day
- Cook rather than living on snacks (then again, do what you wish. God knows I did for 25 years)
- Do the best that you can, when you can
- Try out a lot of probiotics if the first ones don't work
- Protect your future brain health through a healthy diet
- Find what works for you
- Focus on nutrient density over calories in food
- Focus on what you add to your diet rather than what you take out of it
- When it comes to exercise, simplify and conquer
- Freeze your bananas.

Chapter 26
What This Book Has Taught You About Life

- Don't send your laughing cousin to the psych ward
- Never underestimate a woman with a scalpel and an uncle who's a butcher
- Get mustard seeds for your farty boyfriend
- Bloat and debloat as you wish
- Don't call a Dr in Psychology when you're having a heart attack
- Don't steal my gut business ideas yet if you make the IBS portable kit with the white noise machine and the lavender spray, do send me a box
- Don't steal my gut business ideas; yet if you cure celiac, do give me a call
- Make healthy diet coke and I will marry you
- If you're a non-native speaker, don't be afraid to use your Engl-ish
- Life's too short to be fully vegan, eat the meringues
- A little bit better is how you get to a lot better

- Don't bring up My Big Fat Greek Wedding in the presence of Greeks unless you're one of them
- Kiss your brutally honest friends goodbye
- Don't blow out your ruptured eardrums when at work
- Better marry a psychiatrist than a hands-on/hands-in doctor
- Better speak in gut-infested jargon to stir shit up.
- P.S. If you even acknowledge me in a public space, don't mention I wrote this book. I'm a lady for God's sake! I don't speak gut ;)

Notes

Chapter 2

1. Maranki, J., & Stavropoulos, S. N. (2019). Endoscopic Full-Thickness Resection of Subepithelial Lesions of the GI Tract. Clinical Gastrointestinal Endoscopy. doi:10.1016/b978-0-323-41509-5.00046-3

2. Moszak, M; Szulińska, M; Bogdański, P (2020 April, 15). "You Are What You Eat – The Relationship between Diet, Microbiota, and Metabolic Disorders- A Review". Nutrients. 12 (4): 1096. doi:10.3390/nu12041096

3. Wang, Y., & Kasper, L. H. (2014). The role of microbiome in central nervous system disorders. Brain, behavior, and immunity, 38, 1–12. https://doi.org/10.1016/j.bbi.2013.12.015

4. Cryan, J.F., Dinan, T.G., 2012. Mind-altering microorganisms: the impact of the gut microbiota on brain and behaviour. Nat. Rev. Neurosci. 13, 701–712.

5. Mayer, E.A., Tillisch, K., Gupta, A., 2015. Gut/brain axis and the microbiota. J. Clin. Invest. 125, 926–938.

6. Romijn, J.A., Corssmit, E.P., Havekes, L.M., Pijl, H., 2008. Gut-brain axis. Curr. Opin. Clin. Nutr. Metab. Care 11, 518–521.

7. Sender, R., Fuchs, S., Milo, R., 2016. Revised Estimates for the Number of Human and Bacteria Cells in the Body. PLoS Biol. 14, 1–14.

8. Dinan, T.G., Cryan, J.F., 2017. Gut–brain axis in 2016: Brain–gut–microbiota axis – mood, metabolism and behaviour. Nat. Rev. Gastroenterol. Hepatol.

9. Strandwitz P. (2018). Neurotransmitter modulation by the gut microbiota. *Brain research*, *1693*(Pt B), 128–133. https://doi.org/10.1016/j.brainres.2018.03.015

10. Evrensel, A., & Ceylan, M. E. (2015). The Gut-Brain Axis: The Missing Link in Depression. *Clinical psychopharmacology and neuroscience: the official scientific journal of the Korean College of Neuropsychopharmacology*, *13*(3), 239–244. https://doi.org/10.9758/cpn.2015.13.3.239

Chapter 3

11. Katherine D. McManus, M. (2019, February 27). Should I be eating more fiber? Retrieved from https://www.health.harvard.edu/blog/should-i-be-eating-more-fiber2019022115927#:~:text=On average, American adults eat,and 30 daily grams, respectively.

12. Dreher, M. L. (2015). Role of Fiber and Healthy Dietary Patterns in Body Weight Regulation and

131

Weight Loss. Advances in Obesity, Weight Management & Control, 3(5). doi:10.15406/aowmc.2015.03.00068

13. Mickelsen, O., Makdani, D. D., Cotton, R. H., Titcomb, S. T., Colmey, J. C., & Gatty, R. (1979). Effects of a high fiber bread diet on weight loss in college-age males. The American Journal of Clinical Nutrition, 32(8), 1703-1709. doi:10.1093/ajcn/32.8.1703

14. Crumbs... How a loaf a day will make you thin. (2005, October 15). Retrieved from https://www.theguardian.com/uk/2005/oct/16/health.foodanddrink

15. Han, Y., & Xiao, H. (2020). Whole Food–Based Approaches to Modulating Gut Microbiota and Associated Diseases. Annual Review of Food Science and Technology, 11(1), 119-143. doi:10.1146/annurev-food-111519-014337

16. Pellegrini, N., & Fogliano, V. (2017). Cooking, industrial processing and caloric density of foods. Current Opinion in Food Science, 14, 98-102. doi:10.1016/j.cofs.2017.02.006

Chapter 4

17. Mantantzis, K., Schlaghecken, F., Sünram-Lea, S. I., & Maylor, E. A. (2019). Sugar rush or sugar crash? A meta-analysis of carbohydrate effects on mood. Neuroscience & Biobehavioral Reviews, 101, 45-67. doi:10.1016/j.neubiorev.2019.03.016

Chapter 5

18. Alang, N., & Kelly, C. R. (2015). Weight Gain After Fecal Microbiota Transplantation. Open Forum Infectious Diseases, 2(1). doi:10.1093/ofid/ofv004

19. Kang, Y., & Cai, Y. (2017). Gut microbiota and obesity: Implications for fecal microbiota transplantation therapy. Hormones, 16(3), 223-234. doi:10.1007/bf03401517

20. Kao, D., & Surawicz, C. (2020). Fecal Microbiota Transplant. Encyclopedia of Gastroenterology, 431-435. doi:10.1016/b978-0-12-801238-3.65954-8.

Chapter 6

21. Diet Myths · Podcast · deliciously ella. (n.d.). Retrieved from https://deliciouslyella.com/podcast/diet-myths/

Chapter 7

22. Desjardins, E. (2016). The Urban Food Desert. Imagining Sustainable Food Systems, 87-112. doi:10.4324/9781315587905-6

23. Warde, A. (2012). The Reconstruction of Taste in Consumption, Food and Taste: Culinary Antinomies and Commodity Culture Consumption, Food and Taste: Culinary Antinomies and Commodity Culture, 157-179. doi:10.4135/9781446222027.n9

24. Provasi, S. (2017). Gut bacteria and Alzheimer's disease: From dysbiosis to betaamyloid plaques.

doi:10.26226/morressier.5971be86d462b80290b527
f6

25. Geng, M. (2020). Causal communication between gut
microbiota dysbiosis and neuroinflammation in
Alzheimer's disease and therapeutic intervention by
oligomannate. Alzheimers & Dementia, 16(S2).
doi:10.1002/alz.044151.

Chapter 13

26. Ramachandran, V. S., & Blakeslee, S. (2009).
Phantoms in the brain: Probing the mysteries of the
human mind. New York: Harper Perennial.

27. Bushara, K. O. (2005). Neurologic presentation of
celiac disease. Gastroenterology, 128(4).
doi:10.1053/j.gastro.2005.02.018

28. Yamashiro, K., Tanaka, R., Urabe, T., Ueno, Y.,
Yamashiro, Y., Nomoto, K., Hattori, N. (2017). Gut
dysbiosis is associated with metabolism and systemic
inflammation in patients with ischemic stroke. Plos
One, 12(2). doi:10.1371/journal.pone.0171521

29. Treangen, T. J., Wagner, J., Burns, M. P., & Villapol,
S. (2018). Traumatic Brain Injury in Mice Induces
Acute Bacterial Dysbiosis Within the Fecal
Microbiome. Frontiers in Immunology, 9.
doi:10.3389/fimmu.2018.02757

30. Simela Chatzikonstantinou, Georgia Gioula, Vasilios
K. Kimiskidis, Jack McKenna, Ioannis Mavroudis, &
Dimitrios Kazis. (2021). The gut microbiome in drug-
resistant epilepsy. Epilepsia Open, 6(1), 28–37.
https://doihttps://doi-

org.avoserv2.library.fordham.edu/10.1002/epi4.
12461org.avoserv2.library.fordham.edu/10.1002/epi
4.12461

31. Dahlin, M., & Prast-Nielsen, S. (2019). The gut
microbiome and epilepsy. EBioMedicine, 44, 741-
746.
doi:https://doi.org/10.1016/j.ebiom.2019.05.024

32. Allum, W. H., Griffin, S. M., Watson, A., & Colin-
Jones, D. (2011). Guidelines for the management of
oesophageal and gastric cancer. Gut, 50 Suppl 5, v1-
23. https://doi-
org.avoserv2.library.fordham.edu/10.1136/gut.5
0.suppl_5.v1org.avoserv2.library.fordham.edu/10.1
136/gut.50.suppl_5.v1

33. O'Keefe, S. J., Kidd, M., Espitalier-Noel, G., &
Owira, P. (1999). Rarity of colon cancer in Africans
is associated with low animal product consumption,
not fiber. The American journal of gastroenterology,
94(5), 1373–1380. https://doi.org/10.1111/j.1572-
0241.1999.01089.x

34. Sona Ciernikova, Michal Mego, & Michal Chovanec.
(2021). Exploring the Potential Role of the Gut
Microbiome in Chemotherapy-Induced
Neurocognitive Disorders and Cardiovascular
Toxicity. Cancers, 13 (782), 782.
https://doihttps://doi-
org.avoserv2.library.fordham.edu/10.3390/canc
ers13040782org.avoserv2.library.fordham.edu/10.3
390/cancers13040782

35. LaChance, L. R., & Ramsey, D. (2018). Antidepressant foods: An evidence-based nutrient profiling system for depression. World journal of psychiatry, 8(3), 97–104. https://doi.org/10.5498/wjp.v8.i3.97

36. Aslam, H., Green, J., Jacka, F. N., Collier, F., Berk, M., Pasco, J., & Dawson, S. L. (2020). Fermented foods, the gut and mental health: a mechanistic overview with implications for depression and anxiety. Nutritional Neuroscience, 23(9), 659–671. https://doi-org.avoserv2.library.fordham.edu/10.1080/1028415X.2018.1544332

37. Benton, D., & Cook, R. (1991). The impact of selenium supplementation on mood. Biological Psychiatry, 29(11),https://doihttps://doi-org.avoserv2.library.fordham.edu/10.1016/0006-3223(91)90251-Gorg.avoserv2.library.fordham.edu/10.1016/0006-3223(91)90251-G

38. Sanchez-Villegas, A., Henríquez, P., Figueiras, A., Ortuño, F., Lahortiga, F., & Martínez-González, M. A. (2007). Long chain omega-3 fatty acids intake, fish consumption and mental disorders in the SUN cohort study. European Journal of Nutrition, 46(6), 337. https://doi-org.avoserv2.library.fordham.edu/10.1007/s00394-007-0671-x

39. Zhang, W.-H., Liu, W.-Z., He, Y., You, W.-J., Zhang, J.-Y., Xu, H., Tian, X.-L., Li, B.-M., Mei, L., Holmes, A., & Pan, B.-X. (2019). Chronic Stress Causes

ProjectionSpecific Adaptation of Amygdala Neurons via Small-Conductance Calcium-Activated Potassium Channel Downregulation. Biological Psychiatry, 85(10), 812–828. https://doiorg.avoserv2.library.fordham.edu/10.1016/j.biopsych.2018.12.010

40. Esmaily, H., Sahebkar, A., Iranshahi, M., Ganjali, S., Mohammadi, A., Ferns, G., & Ghayour-Mobarhan, M. (2015). An investigation of the effects of curcumin on anxiety and depression in obese individuals: A randomised controlled trial. Chinese Journal of Integrative Medicine, 21(5), 332. https://doihttps://doi-org.avoserv2.library.fordham.edu/10.1007/s116 55-015-2160-zorg.avoserv2.library.fordham.edu/10.1007/s11655-015-2160-z

41. E. Georgousopoulou, D.D. Mellor, N. Naumovski, D. Panagiotakos, C. Chrysohoou, N. Skourlis, D. Tousoulis, C. Stefanadis, & C. Pitsavos. (2017). Anxiety levels moderate the protective effect of dark chocolate polyphenol intake against metabolic syndrome: The ATTICA study. Journal of Nutrition & Intermediary Metabolism, 8(C), 97. https://doi-org.avoserv2.library.fordham.edu/10.1016/j.jnim.20 17.04.139

42. Hilimire, M. R., DeVylder, J. E., & Forestell, C. A. (2015). Fermented foods, neuroticism, and social anxiety: An interaction model. Psychiatry research, 228(2), 203–208. https://doi.org/10.1016/j.psychres.2015.04.023